Whisky Class

PURE MALT WHISKY STORIES

63,5 extraordinary
single malt stories

Fernand
Dacquin

Lannoo

SILVER SEAL
SPEYSIDE SINGLE MALT SCOTCH WHISKY
12
ROYAL LOCHNAGAR
HIGHLAND SINGLE MALT SCOTCH WHISKY
12 YEARS
The MACALLAN
HIGHLAND SINGLE MALT SCOTCH WHISKY
12
DOUBLE CASK
The MACALLAN
SIENNA
HIGHLAND SINGLE MALT SCOTCH WHISKY
GLENMORANGIE
HIGHLAND SINGLE MALT SCOTCH WHISKY
The ORIGINAL
GLENMORANGIE
HIGHLAND SINGLE MALT SCOTCH WHISKY
The QUINTA RUBAN
EXTRA MATURED IN PORT CASKS
12
GLENMORANGIE
HIGHLAND SINGLE MALT SCOTCH WHISKY
THE GLENLIVET
15
THE GLENLIVET
SINGLE MALT SCOTCH WHISKY
18
TORMORE
SINGLE SPEYSIDE MALT
AGED 12 YEARS
AGED 16 YEARS
THE BENRIACH
SINGLE MALT SCOTCH WHISKY
TOMINTOUL
16 YEARS
SPEYSIDE GLENLIVET
PRODUCT OF SCOTLAND
anCnoc
12
anCnoc
16
LONGMORN
16
STRATHISLA
12
Aberfeldy
12
EDRADOUR
EDRADOUR
10
CALEDONIA
EDRADOUR
HIGHLAND SINGLE MALT SCOTCH WHISKY
Aged 12 Years
NATURAL COLOUR
UNCHILLFILTERED
Dalwhinnie
HIGHLAND SINGLE MALT SCOTCH WHISKY
15

Contents

Intro

63.5

Years ago, I asked my good friend Jan Filliers, fifth-generation scion in a family of distillers and himself master distiller at the Filliers Grain Distillery in Deinze (Belgium), why he matured his distillate at 63.5% ABV. He replied without much thought: “Because my grandfather said so!”

Jan was a clever brewer and an experienced distiller. I often enjoyed tasting with him and arguing amicably afterwards about flavours, techniques and the new tricks he had tried. Interestingly, Jan had a poor opinion of ‘wood management’. He attributed the quality of his new spirit more to the distilling process itself than to what happened in the barrels. Sadly, Jan is gone now, but the 63.5% ABV has lingered on. This is true not only in the Filliers grain distillery but also in many other distilleries worldwide. As a result, you will find in all self-respecting whisky books that 63.5% ABV is ‘the calibrated measure at which new spirit should be matured in the whisky industry’.

Ah, if things were really that simple.

More than twenty-two million barrels of whisky mature in Scotland, with varying results. Two neighbouring, seemingly identical casks, filled with the same new spirit at 63.5% ABV, will sometimes produce two completely different whiskies after a few years.

Putting whisky in casks with more than 62.5% ABV is forbidden in the United States. In Taiwan, they stay just below 60% to escape stricter fire regulations at higher levels. Ireland and Scotland (and many other whisky countries) take liberties with this ‘golden rule’: Aberlour and Highland Park, to name but a few, aim a little higher, and Bruichladdich goes over 70% ABV because Jim McEwan realised that using less water provided more room for alcohol while maturing.

In the past, however, freshly filled whisky casks were often swapped with casks from other distilleries.

By filling all casks to the same strength, they avoided complex conversions when calculating prices.

Instead, they opted for an easy-to-remember number: 111 degrees proof, based on the old measuring system. And that's reflected in the new ABV system:63.5% ABV.

That is why I keep insisting on this 'ideal 63.5'; it is a number with a whisky history, and therefore, it undoubtedly belongs in a whisky book.

So we'll stick with 63.5%.

All that remains is the pressing question: how do you write half a chapter? Do I write a whole piece and dump the end? Or do I remove the middle section? Skipping the intro seems stupid.

I'll find out; I need to write 63 chapters first.

We'll see.

1 Barleycorn

I don't need to explain what 'barley' is to whisky lovers. No barley, no whisky or 'juice of the barley', as Robbie Burns passionately called 'malt whisky'. Romantics, those Scots. But you must be very romantic about using 'one grain of barley' as a measure of length.

But believe me, a 'barleycorn' is definitely the length of a grain of barley, even by royal decree.

'One barley corne dry and rounde' was literally written in the decree issued by King Edward II in 1324, who wanted to establish the standard measures in his kingdom once and for all.

What a concept! The brains behind this stroke of genius had certainly never seen barley before, or they had been drinking too much whisky. Barley grains are like zebras: they all look more or less the same, but it is hard to find two identical ones. There are more than five hundred varieties of barley, and new strains are continuously being added. For instance, there is two-row barley, with fairly regular grains, but also six-row barley, with grains that take on the craziest shapes.

Now it's up to you: how long do you think a grain of barley is?

Well, it's easy: the law of 1324 also says that a row of three grains of barley 'laid lengthwise' is one inch long. See how easy it is?

But wait: at that time, an 'inch' was defined as 'the width of a thumb measured at the base of the nail'... And thumbs are like zebras... etc.

We haven't made any progress at all.

Fortunately, the British are much more level-headed today than back in 1324. Since 1 July 1959, only imperial units have been used in the UK (and the USA), and they clearly state that one inch is 25.4 mm.

Voilà: 25.4 mm divided by 3 is 8.47 mm. So, the law states that one barleycorn is exactly 8.47 mm everywhere.

Look, another good thing about reading this: from now on, anyone – wherever you come from – can buy shoes in the UK (where shoe sizes are measured using barleycorn) without a problem.

This is essential for my non-British and non-American readers: you must remember that a 'UK size 12 men's shoe' is precisely 12 inches. And you know already: 12 inches is 36 barleycorn or 305 mm.

But... this '12 inches' is not the length of the shoe, but the 'length of the foot': from the tip of the longest toe to the heel, measured in millimetres. A foot length of 305 millimetres corresponds to a non-UK size of 47 or 47.5. The rest is easy: subtract one barleycorn for each smaller UK size! So, UK size 10 is 305 mm minus 8.47 mm minus 8.47 mm or 288 mm.

Voilà, simple, isn't it? What could possibly go wrong?

Come on, let's go shoe shopping in Edinburgh. Don't panic... I'll stay with you.

BARLEYCORN

WHAT
English measure of length

MEANING
The length of one grain of barley

USAGE
It is only used for shoe sizes in the UK and a few other English-speaking countries

What is your shoe size? 42? OK. Ouch... I need to know the length of your foot, from the tip of your longest toe to the heel, in millimetres. You don't know that by heart? I expected that, but as you might have guessed, I have the answer: divide your shoe size by 0.15 and then subtract 15 mm. In your case, your foot length is 265 mm. All that remains is subtracting 265 from 305 and dividing the result by 8.47. Then we know how many barleycorns to subtract from 12. And that's how we know your UK shoe size: 8 or 8.5.

Well, that's solved satisfactorily!

And now, to my many readers who are also shoe retailers in the UK: if you see one of us in your shop struggling with the most complicated calculations, help us! Please show us your little conversion table with the two shoe size systems side by side. We'll be out in an instant, and two minutes later, we'll be in the pub next to your shoe shop with a wee dram in front of us.

There will be much less calculation involved.

But now that I've unlocked the mathematical knot that's been dormant in the back of your mind for so long, I'm sure the same question is going through your head as it did mine: while I am writing this, I've got 5 centilitres of whisky at 40% ABV in front of me. How many barleycorns did it take to make?

Well, I worked it out for you. (To keep it simple, I'm going to use very rounded numbers from now on.)

A 'Thousand Grains Weight' of barley (a measure that really exists, mind you) is 40 grams. So a thousand grains of barley weigh 40 grams. Therefore, one tonne of barley contains 25,000,000 grains. One tonne of barley gives us 400 litres of pure alcohol. With this, we can make 1,000 bottles of 1 litre at 40% ABV.

Therefore, I need 25,000 grains for one bottle and 1,250 grains for one glass (5 centilitres).

Come on, let's lay out those 1,250 grains, as the law of 1324 says, 'lengthwise' one after the other, and we get 1,250 times 8.47 mm = 10,587.5 mm.

That's about 10.60 metres.

Ten metres! It's not that far, is it?

You see, 5 centilitres of whisky is a small whisky indeed!

Barley grains are like zebras:
they all look more or less the same,
but it is hard to find two identical ones.

2 Welsh whisky

> WELSH WHISKY
> QUESTION
> Do we attribute 'whisky' to the Irish? The Scots? Or the Welsh?
> OUR CONTENTION
> Welshmen claim to be the very first whisky distillers
> OUR WITNESS
> Taliesin

When Alfred Bernard visited all the distilleries in Britain in 1886–1887, he finished off the Welsh distilleries in one fell swoop. There were none left! Someone made a bold start shortly afterwards, but the story was over again twenty years later. Prohibition had nipped it in the bud.

But the Welsh were not sad. In fact, they boast that their whisky history goes back further than that of Ireland or Scotland.

You only have to tell us once, and we look for proof. We can't resist the urge.

And behold!

In the second half of the sixth century, at the court of King Urien of Rheged in Wales, there lived a bard renowned for his talents in song and word: Taliesin was his name. We know little about the good man, except that he was still regarded as one of Britain's greatest poets centuries later. That may be why his songs and poems were passed down from generation to generation. In the 14th century, for example, a booklet entitled 'Llyfr Taliesin' or 'The Book of Taliesin' appeared, containing 57 of his poems in Welsh. Thankfully, some brave soul later translated them all into English, but Taliesin's surprising imagery doesn't make you much wiser. Slaloming through his verses requires some imagination.

In his long poem 'Angar Kyfyndawt', which roughly translates as 'The Enemy Confederacy', I stumbled through such sequences as

I have been a stock,
I have been a spade,
I have been an axe in the hand;
I have been a needle in tweezers,
A year and a half;
I've been a speckled white rooster
With chickens in Eiddyn.

I admit I lasted only a short time, unlike Stuart McHardy. Stuart is a celebrated Scottish writer, researcher, musician, poet and storyteller. He went through the whole poem and snagged on a few lines near the end:

I am a grain discovered,
That grew on a hill.
The man mowed me,
Drained me of my juices,
In a room full of smoke.

It is generally accepted that the poet was alluding here to the use of hallucinogenic mushrooms. Bards seem to have indulged in magic mushrooms at the time.

But Stuart McHardy did not fall for it. Although he can often be hilarious, he takes the following conclusion very seriously: the 'grain on the hill' is 'barley'; these 'juices' refer to the sugary 'wort' filtered from the barley; and this 'room full of smoke' puts us in a Welsh hut, without windows or a chimney, where a primitive still is glowing on a peat fire, slowly spitting out a clear 'new spirit'. Here, whisky is distilled.

Conclusion: Wales was first. It was not the Irish who brought whisky to Scotland, but the Welsh! In the sixth century! And they taught it to the Picts who lived there.

Just forget once and for all that we learnt distilling from the Arabs about a thousand years ago.

But wait, not so fast.

The question now is: were these Picts eagerly awaiting this import? Perhaps they already had a distillate of their own that preceded the Welsh! Unfortunately, we know very little about the Picts, not even their actual names; we are still determining what they called themselves. Apart from some beautifully carved stones, almost nothing remains of them.

Except for the name 'Heather Yill'.

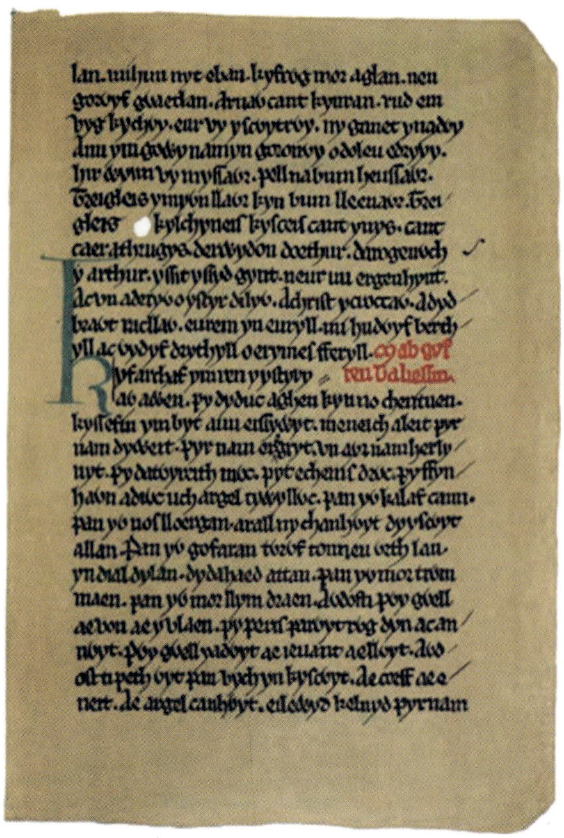

Llyfr Taliesin →

According to legend, as early as the fifth century, the Picts were brewing a secret drink that they called, misleadingly, Heather Yill. The recipe was top secret, and the reference to heather was only there to deceive the enemy. After all, Heather Yill gave the warriors strength and courage, something that could also be co-opted by the enemy.

In a battle in what is now Dumfries & Galloway, the Scots, who had come over from Ireland, captured several Picts. Among them were an older man and his son. The Scots told the man that they would kill him and his son if he did not give them Heather Yill's recipe. The father, knowing they would kill them anyway, suggested they kill his son first, and then he would reveal the secret. That way, the son would not witness his father's weakness and betrayal. They did so.

But when they got to the father after killing the son, he refused to reveal the secret.

"I did not want my boy to see me die," he said proudly. And he, too, was killed.

Tell me honestly, for what drink would you go as far as that father?

That's not difficult to imagine. There is only one!

So that means the Picts might have been first...

↓ Snowdonia National Park, Wales

3 What Is a Tot?

> WHAT IS A TOT?
>
> WHAT
>
> Old British measure of volume, often a source of confusion
>
> SIZE
>
> Nobody knows exactly how big a tot is. The term is similar to a 'lump' of butter or a 'handful' of nuts.
>
> USE
>
> Tot, as a measure of volume, is often used in the context of whisky, such as *'porridge with a tot of whisky'.*

But as a whisky enthusiast, have you ever wondered what a 'tot' of whisky is? Is it 2 centilitres, 5, 10 or more?

Let's delve into this intriguing topic.

In his excellent reference work, 'A to Z of Whisky', Gavin D. Smith explains, "A 'tot' is a small quantity of whisky or other alcoholic liquor...".

Well, with all due respect to Gavin, who is undoubtedly one of the foremost whisky writers, but (for a start) 'small whisky' is a pleonasm. Like 'white snow' or 'green grass'. You're saying the same thing twice. Surely every seasoned whisky drinker knows: EVERY whisky IS a 'small whisky'.

So that doesn't get us anywhere.

Fortunately, we have Stanley Ager's wisdom to guide us. A retired butler with fifty-three years of distinguished service, including to the esteemed Lord Coventry and his daughter Lady Barbara Smith, Ager is a respected authority in his field. He trained many of the butlers who have graced Buckingham Palace and other distinguished places. If anyone knows, it's him.

In his textbook, 'The Butler's Guide to Clothes Care, Managing Table, Running the Home and Other Graces', he puts it very clearly on page 112: "...an inch of whisky is a respectful measure in any glass".

He added that he only poured less whisky if he noticed the guest shaking.

After careful consideration and consultation with the esteemed Stanley Ager, we have finally unravelled the mystery. A tot is 'an inch', he says, literally. At least that is clear.

An inch is 2.54 centimetres. And because he adds 'in any glass', we know he means height. So it's up to us to choose the width of our jar.

Solved...

But of course, you want to know more.

You're probably wondering, 'Isn't a centimetre of whisky too much to drink at breakfast?'

Be careful! You don't have to drink this whisky. On the contrary, you should pour it into the porridge. Yes, whisky lover, you may shudder at the thought of pouring whisky anywhere but down your throat, but let me explain what porridge is, and you will understand.

Porridge, 'the backbone of any tough Scot', is oatmeal or oat grains cooked painfully slowly in a mixture of milk and water and stirred continuously clockwise with a 'spurtle', not a spoon! A spurtle is simply a wooden stick.

Some add salt, others sugar, syrup, cinnamon....

The result looks like clotted wallpaper glue. But it is low in calories and lowers cholesterol.

And it tastes pretty good. I wouldn't say that porridge is my favourite breakfast, but it does have one big plus: no matter what you add, it only gets better.

So sacrificing a whisky is no crime.

Of course, you can always ask for two 'tots' with your porridge to ease the pain. One to pour and...

Stanley Ager's friend George Summers used to ask for three tots. He was the Duke of Buccleuch's gamekeeper and would pop into Stanley Ager's after work for a chat and a couple of tots. Just before leaving, he would always ask for three tots: one in each of his boots and one down the back of his neck. This, he claimed, kept him warm on the journey home.

Note: 'A tot of whisky' should not be confused with 'a finger...', 'a nip...', 'a dram...', 'a slug...' or 'a sniffer' of whisky. These are other critical British measures of volume that we will talk about later.

4 Cambus

"As we passed in the train from the Bridge of Allan to Cambus, the sun, hitherto obscured, suddenly shone forth, pouring down its golden light upon the scene, bringing out in bold relief each crag and pinnacle, and casting fantastic shadows on the wooded slopes below, relieving the former of their wild ruggedness, and rendering to the latter an air of peaceful repose. For once we could not regret that our locomotion was slow, and that the train stopped at every station, otherwise we might have lost the view of the Wallace Monument, standing on a crag 560 feet above the level of the plain, the Links of the Forth, and the swelling hills each with their rich groupings of scenery, intersected here and there with farmhouses... Just before arriving at the station we crossed the Devon, a river of sparkling beauty, which flows into the Forth at Cambus Distillery.

"This distillery was founded in the year 1806 by John Moubray, the grandfather of one of the Directors of the Company... Originally a small work, it has now grown to enormous dimensions... The buildings are spread over fully eight acres of ground and are everywhere intersected by the railway."

CAMBUS

WHAT

Name of a distillery in Clackmannanshire, in the Lowlands. Name of accompanying whiskies.

PRODUCED

Malt and grain whiskies

SIGNIFICANCE

Behind two significant events in the history of Scotch whisky

We are in 1886, and the above musings were penned by Alfred Barnard, who was in the middle of writing his masterpiece 'The Whisky Distilleries of the United Kingdom'.

He must have been quite impressed, not only with the countryside around Stirling but certainly also with the Cambus distillery. He meticulously describes all the buildings, stills, pots and pans found there and ends his account with the all-important final line: "There are seven excise officers at the distillery." So one was apparently not enough.

The distillery was indeed one of the big ones. Founded 1806 as a small malt distillery, Cambus installed a prototype 'Robert Stein column still' in 1827. This provided a continuous supply of alcohol but did not produce the desired results. Four years later, Aeneas Coffee patented a much-improved version: a good, constant process with a high alcohol content that could use raw materials other than grain. This system convinced Cambus. In 1836, he installed two of Coffee's stills. But they were not alone in this: Scotland, England, Ireland and even Germany and Belgium switched to the column still.

At first, no one in Scotland saw anything wrong with it. The blenders eagerly took up the 'new' alcohol they distilled in the column stills, and Cambus even exported a lot of it to England, where it was further processed and used in gin and other applications.

But in 1848, the British legislature came up with a great idea: in Scotland, only cereals could be used for distilling, while any agricultural products could be used in England. This was a kick in the teeth for Cambus.

Along with five other large lowland grain distillers, they decided to fight back. In 1856, they formed a consortium that, by 1877, would become the Distillers

CAMBUS DISTILLERY.

Cambus was praised for its quality not only by blenders, but also by consumers.

Company Limited or DCL, which became hugely important in British whisky.

Their ultimate goal was jointly controlling prices, quantities, promotions and discounts on grain alcohol. They quickly became the most significant player in the UK whisky market, and their influence continued to grow. In 1997, after various mergers and several acquisitions, DCL became drinks giant Diageo. By that time, the whole whisky world could no longer ignore it: Diageo is the world's largest drinks company, operating in 180 countries with over 30,000 employees. The multinational owns 28 malt distilleries and several grain distilleries in Scotland. Cambus had been one of those, but its previous owner, Guinness, had already decided to close down and phase out production at Cambus in 1993. Diageo eventually established a cooperage in the old buildings.

Cambus was praised for its quality not only by blenders, but also by consumers. Cambus was the first to bottle and sell 'single grain' column alcohol.

In 1906, DCL even marketed a seven-year-old Cambus grain whisky as the figurehead for an expensive but crucial advertising campaign. An advertisement for 'Cambus grain whisky' appeared on the front page of the Daily Mail with the telling headline: 'Not a headache in a gallon'. This was an invitation for readers to discover that grain whisky was authentic and delicious, too.

It would become a standard phrase in marketing language.

This advertisement was the battering ram that the grain distillers would use in a legal battle against the malt distillers. A fight to the death! The famous 'what is whisky?' case.

Spoiler... the grain distillers won. Thanks to Cambus?

5 Mount Vernon Distillery

MOUNT VERNON DISTILLERY

WHAT
US President George Washington's estate

WHERE
Near Alexandria, Virginia

SIGNIFICANCE
Once the largest distillery in the United States

They worked for days on that damned text, weighing each word three times, arguing, shouting and threatening, adjusting where they could, reckoning with the wishes of yet another pesky delegate from yet another one of those twelve colonies, rehashing it all out loud, and then, with everyone nodding, very satisfied, almost in unison, they put down their brand-new pens. They had finally completed the text of one of the most significant documents in human history: the new Constitution of the United States of America. The year was 1787.

Undoubtedly, someone must have stood up and shouted, "Gentlemen, let's have a drink!"

Chances are that it was none other than George Washington, the very first President of the freshly forged USA. He must not have encountered much opposition: if you look at the original document of the 'Constitution', you cannot ignore some traces of a less than steady hand in the signatures. The 'Founding Fathers' of the United States were anything but teetotallers; we would now call them 'drunkards'. Taking the lead in all matters, Washington seized every opportunity to throw a party.

On 14 September, three days before the signing of the Constitution, he held a dinner party with 55 guests, including members of the Philadelphia City Cavalry. The list of empty bottles from that evening speaks for itself: 60 bottles of red wine, 54 bottles of Madeira, 8 bottles of cider, 8 bottles of whisky, 22 bottles of stout, 12 (small) kegs of light beer and 7 bowls of punch.

In those days, no one thought twice about such an astounding amount. Around 1800, the average alcohol consumption in the United States was 27 litres of pure alcohol per person per year. That's a lot! But all these drinks were safer than water, and some were even cheaper than tea or coffee. In the minds of the new Americans, they were categorised as 'food' rather than 'drink'.

Alcohol was daily fare.

President Washington's successor, John Adams, drank three glasses of Madeira before breakfast to rinse his mouth and consumed a good deal of rum and wine before bed. George Washington had a similar habit, which he continued steadily throughout the day.

To this day, evil tongues claim that good old George was a drunkard!

Why is that? Because he drank a bottle of Madeira daily, supplemented by rum and punch? Or because his accounts show that in the last six months of 1775, he bought six hundred dollars' worth of liquor (about 16,000 British pounds today)?

Or because he gave his gardener an extra month's pay at Christmas and Easter and a permit to come to work drunk four times a year? George, a drunkard? Come on. What are you talking about?

Ah yes, it's said that his wooden dentures had to be replaced several times because they rotted from drinking! But that's just 'fake news': although he did in fact have several sets of dentures, none were made of wood. They were all made of metal (often gold), inlaid with first-class cattle teeth or little jewels carved from ivory. Proof of this is in his last set of dentures, which is on display in the historic Mount Vernon estate museum.

I hope I have completely cleared poor George's record.

President Washington died in 1799 – not from cirrhosis of the liver, but from the consequences of a respiratory infection. He came home from his estate that night soaking wet but kept his wet clothes on (which was a terrible idea even then) and got up the next day with a sore throat. His health got worse and worse, and the doctors decided to treat him by bloodletting. One session turned into two and then three... Once they had drained almost four litres of blood, they were about to suggest trying something else, but he suddenly dropped dead. Even a president has no more than five litres of blood, and that last remaining litre turned out not to be enough.

In 1797, George Washington established a distillery at his Mount Vernon estate in Virginia. It was the largest in America at the time, boasting five stills. The distillery was not solely for Washington's personal consumption, as he produced more than 40,000 litres shortly before his death. This production amount surpassed the other 3,500 distilleries in Virginia, which hardly produced 2,500 litres.

Washington himself knew more about brewing beer than about distilling whisky, as a keen beer drinker. For his whisky, he therefore enlisted the help of a Scottish emigrant, James Anderson, who trained six of Washington's over one hundred slaves to become full-fledged distillers. As a result, their casks (the whisky was sold by cask and had no real brand name) easily found their way to eager customers. James had brought extensive crafting experience to the New World, so he distilled according to a tried-and-tested recipe: 60 per cent rye, 35 per cent corn, and 5 per cent malted barley. And he distilled twice.

This process is still done today at the Mount Vernon distillery, rebuilt in 2007, which has a tasting room.

The `Founding Fathers' of the United States were anything but teetotallers; we would now call them `drunkards'. Taking the lead in all matters, Washington seized every opportunity to throw a party.

A little-known detail in the whole story: George Washington, like all other distillers, received a notice from the tax authorities at the end of the year to pay taxes on the alcohol he produced. He introduced this law himself in 1791, much to the dismay of the entire distilling world. That law, incidentally, led to a veritable people's uprising (later called the Whiskey Rebellion) and an uncontrolled witch-hunt against anyone who had anything to do with these taxes.

In 1794, George Washington was compelled to dispatch a 13,000-strong army to Pennsylvania to quell that rebellion. However, it never led to a battle as none of the rebels showed up on the battlefield. Instead, they all stayed home. The army only managed to capture two passers-by who were later sentenced to death. But President Washington showed his wisdom by pardoning them, proving that he was a clear-headed leader.

In 1798, he paid $332 as tax for his whisky, which would be equivalent to approximately £8500 today. It's often said that history repeats itself, but have you heard of any presidents or heads of state who have dutifully paid taxes on all of their income and assets, like responsible citizens?

The distillery in Mount Vernon →

6 Cornelis Melyn

CORNELIS MELYN

WHO

The first distiller in America

BORN

In the Zakstraat in Antwerp, Belgium.

A DISTILLERY IN KENTUCKY?

Forget it

You've probably never wondered where the first drops of commercial American whiskey, which the Yankees are so proud of, were produced.

It was a long time ago, and you weren't there... but take a guess.

Virginia? Stay serious. Pennsylvania? Nice try. Kentucky? Expected. Tennessee? Forget it.

No, the very first commercially produced American whiskey flowed in the north-eastern corner of Staten Island, New York, in a town still called New Brighton. This small town on the eastern seaboard of the USA was named after Brighton, 'The Kissing City', in the south of England.

And who was the first commercial distiller in America? None other than Cornelis Melyn, a pioneering Flemish entrepreneur!

Cornelis was born in Antwerp's Zakstraat in early September of 1600, a time when Europe was undergoing significant political and social changes. His surname 'Melyn' is said to derive from the city of Malines, or Mechelen in Flemish. We also know that his parents died when he was young and that a half-brother raised him. He was apprenticed to a tailor at a very young age and had become a master tailor by the time he was 17. But that's not where his adventures ended.

Nova Belgica and Nieuw Nederland →

At that point, there was nothing to suggest that this boy would later lead a life that would have repercussions across the ocean.

Less than a year later, in 1618, he went to the church of St Walburga, where he had been baptised, to ask for an extract from the baptismal register, an essential piece of paper that we would now call a 'Certificate of Good Conduct'. This credential allowed him to leave his home country.

He chose the New World as his destination. He would not return until ten years later, mainly to claim an inheritance and to marry Janneke Adriaens, with whom he would have eleven children. The marriage certificate lists him as a 'maker of fine leather'.

Anyway, he was not a man without ideas.

He crossed the ocean a total of twelve times. The fourth time was a winner: the Dutch West India Company, which wanted to lure people to America, was giving away large tracts of land and feudal rights to all who came and brought fifty other fortune-seekers. Bingo for Cornelis.

On arrival, he was granted the rights to almost all of Staten Island. General Willem Kieft, in charge of New Amsterdam, asked him to install a whisky distillery in the buildings of a farmstead destroyed by the local natives.

By now we're in 1641.

New Amsterdam wasn't much back then, no bigger than today's Manhattan. In the early 17th century, it was mostly a vast forest with scattered settlements and a few 'European' houses along the coast.

"The country is excellent and pleasant, full of noble trees and vines, and nothing is lacking except the labour and industry of humans to make it one of the most beautiful and fertile lands in this part of the world..." wrote Johan de Laet in his 1625 book 'Nieuwe Werldt ofte Beschrijvinghe van West-Indien' (The New World or the Description of the West Indies). At that time, New York had a population of around four hundred.

Staten Island was another story: until the arrival of Cornelis Melyn, the few attempts to establish a permanent settlement had failed. The natives made life so difficult for the newcomers that escape was always the only solution.

But Cornelis and his followers got a group of soldiers to provide security. In 1642, he was given the rights to the whole island, with all the authority that came with it.

He could finally start his distillery.

No one knows what his business was like. It must not have been very big, because his market was not very large in scope, especially as it was forbidden to sell alcohol to indigenous populations. The practice was punished by heavy fines and even deportation. Of course, despite this strict rule, it happened anyway – if only to get the natives so drunk that they could be easily cheated and robbed. But that would ultimately lead to the downfall of what we can generously call his New Brighton Distillery.

But the main question is: was he even making whisky at all?

He didn't have much choice; there was plenty of wild fruit growing in the area, and we know (from a letter he wrote to a friend) that he had plenty of plums and juicy grapes. Cereals were also grown, and he could buy plenty of corn (maize) from the local natives. The burgeoning New World also had no shortage of beer, which would become his main raw material. He distilled beer to make what is still called 'white whiskey' in America. We call it 'new spirit' because it rarely spent a single day in a barrel, but was immediately put up for sale. That's what it was intended for. Even today, white whisky is often used in cocktails instead of vodka.

So the answer to "Did he make whisky?" is yes!

As the very first commercial whiskey distiller in America, Cornelis experienced a second novelty: the very first (albeit partial) prohibition in America. Willem Kieft, who would later be succeeded by Peter Stuyvesant, did not like the evildoing of these foreign settlers: from that point on, they were not allowed to sleep with indigenous women (despite protests that there were too few of their own), nor could they buy alcohol during church services and after nine in the evening. However, as was later observed under identical restrictions, the measures didn't help at all.

The distillery's journey was not without its challenges. In 1644, after barely two years of operation, it was attacked and burned down by angry Lenape warriors.

Cornelis Melyn bravely fled to what is now Manhattan, bought himself several houses (so he must have had some savings) and started a new life without whisky.

Deed of Purchase of Staten Island →

7 Water

Whisky enthusiasts often wonder whether adding water to their drink is an excellent way to enhance its flavour. If so, what kind of water should they use? This dilemma can cause stress and sleepless nights for true whisky lovers. However, we have the answer to this age-old question.

We will go into this in more detail later, of course, but first some critical observations:

1. There is a water shortage in the world!
2. The Apostle Paul wrote an admonishing letter to his disciple Timothy about two thousand years ago, clearly stating that Timothy should stop drinking water!
   And Paul became HOLY, lol.
   (Because I can hear you sighing, "Oh goodie... two thousand years ago, but we're living in the twenty-first century!"... wait and listen to this.)
3. In 1854, cholera broke out in London, in the Soho district. More than five hundred people died within a week. A local doctor, John Snow, drew a map of the area with a black stripe for each dead person at each house. He discovered that most of the deaths occurred in and around Broad Street, so the cause of this disaster had to be somewhere there. Indeed, a communal water pump on the corner of Broad Street and Cambridge Street was the culprit. Anyone who drank from the pump became irrevocably ill.

A small brewery and distillery were located nearby. Interestingly, the distillery workers did not experience any health issues. How was this possible?

> WATER
> WHAT
> A colourless and tasteless liquid
> IMPORTANT
> "No rain, no whisky!" This Scottish saying underlines the importance of water in whisky.
> WHY
> Before, during and after distillation, water plays a crucial role in whisky! Or am I exaggerating?

As you can imagine, they had other liquids to drink.

But I don't want to frighten anyone. You can drink water safely these days!

Mark Twain once said, "Water in moderation can do no harm." He was right, but the balance should not tip the other way.

I'll freely admit that I have drunk water before, so I know what I'm talking about. Believe me: no need to do it for the taste.

But in the whisky world, water is often hailed with reverence, and rightly so! We would be lost without it. Take a bottle of whisky, 70 centilitres at 40% ABV. That means 28 centilitres of it is alcohol. Producing those 28 centilitres takes a whopping 13 litres of water! And that's not including all the water used in the condensers.

So, to answer the first water-related question, "How much water do we need?" Plenty, lots of, sometimes more than we have. And if we don't have enough, the master distiller and his people can simply stay home for a few days.

Second question: "What kind of water is best?"

We have many choices: soft or hard water, from spring or river, rain or snow, peat, granite or limestone soil, young or old water, summer or winter water, and so on. It will be a fine anthology.

Forget about it: connoisseurs are increasingly convinced that all of these much-vaunted characteristics have little effect on the flavour of your whisky. If water plays a role in the final product, it is mainly in fermentation. The high acidity in soft water can act more on the yeast, resulting in a shift in flavour – and a little less or more alcohol.

In the event that the European Union, concerned as always for our general welfare, soon decides (as they intend) that we should only use distilled water to make whisky in future, all my writing above will have been for naught.

But now to the vital question: "How much and what kind of water should I add to my whisky?"

Before you read on, make sure you have a whisky in front of you because we are about to get serious. Are you ready? I suppose you could restrain yourself and only pour 5 centilitres.

Let's take a moment to observe: your drink contains 40% ABV, which means that your glass contains 2 centilitres of alcohol and 3 centilitres of water.

WATER!

So, should we add water?

That is not the most critical question; the more important question is: what water is in your glass?

Is it the unique water that flowed over granite and through peat that bubbled up in the spring and was carefully collected and used for fermentation?

The answer is short: we don't know, and the chances are slim.

In Scotland, most whiskies are bottled near Glasgow and Edinburgh, often far from the distillery and the overpowering spring. So, chances are the water added at bottling to bring the ABV down to 40 or 43 is not spring water but tap water from Glasgow or Edinburgh. And there is nothing wrong with that, since Scottish beauties have dissected this water with motherly care in the accompanying laboratories.

So, if you don't have a Scottish beauty at home to dissect your tap water, I recommend using simple bottled water if you want to add a few drops to your glass.

So that's resolved. Now on to: how much water and why?

Let's return to our glass if you still have it; otherwise, we'll wait a moment.

Suppose you want to add five drops of water to your whisky to provoke a reaction.

We know that there are already 3 centilitres of water in your glass. I learned

Mark Twain once said, "Water in moderation can do no harm." He was right, but the balance should not tip the other way.

from a lovely Flemish girlfriend working in a clean room at a laboratory (she will probably read this later) that 1 centilitre of water contains about 200 drops. So there are already 600 drops of water in your glass... and you want to add just 5 drops more!?

It's your whisky, I don't care.

But the question remains: what happens when you add 5 drops of water?

Well, you shake things up: minor chemical reactions suddenly occur between the alcohol and the water, creating energy and slightly raising the temperature of your drink. This increase leads to evaporation. The fruity and floral aromas are the most eager to escape, and you start to smell them quickly; the rest follows slowly. In fact, you will discover more! So... go ahead and do it.

But if you, like me, spent a few years at school, you learned that a liquid that evaporates also cools down; that's how our fridge works. And we know that a drink loses a lot of flavour as it cools.

Conclusion: do me a favour:

Take a second glass and fill it up, too.

Add five drops of water to the first glass, not the second.

Smell both and enjoy.

Wait ten minutes (I know that's a long time), taste both and compare.

And remember what Mark Twain once said: "Whisky is for drinking, water is for fighting over."

The spring from which Glemorangie gets its water ↓

8 Boilermaker

BOILERMAKER

WHAT IT IS

A shot and a beer

EXPLANATION

A 'boilermaker' is what the Dutch call a 'kopstootje', but in this case, with whisky instead of gin.

COMMON

In Britain and the USA

My Uncle Frans was my mother's eldest brother, married to an ever-smiling Aunt Blanche. They remained childless, which was convenient for us (their nieces and nephews). Aunt Blanche gave me twenty francs (ten shillings) in pocket money every Sunday. Uncle Frans didn't care; he was always busy in his workshop. We learned many slang expressions from him that enriched our language. Among other things, he was a highly respected boiler maker. Boilers were needed in all sectors of post-war industry, and Uncle Frans had abundant work. But occasionally, he would 'falter' in the pub. And sometimes, for more than a day. Aunt Blanche always said, "He's working on his 'novena' again." For a boiler maker, much was condoned.

After a long, exhausting day in the scorching heat amidst all the noise, it was pretty natural for these hard workers to crave a refreshing drink: 'a boilermaker', or 'a shot and a beer' as it was called before that. In simpler terms, all you need is a beer and a whisky.

According to the British, this supposed delicacy originated somewhere in Cornwall around 1880; the Americans place it in Montana, where it was initially called a 'Sean O'Farrell' and given to miners at the end of the working day.

The method of drinking is simple: if you drink the whisky first (preferably in one gulp) and then the beer to ease the pain, the beer is called a 'chaser'. There is a second way: slowly pour the whisky into the beer before drinking. But there is also a third method, which I personally think is the best: you take a big sip of your beer first, followed by a second one. Then you take the glass of whisky, hold it in the middle over the beer glass and let it slide down slowly between your fingers so that the glass gently sinks into the beer.

Now, that is the art of drinking. This is where your boilermaker reaches its peak.

At the end of the nineteenth century, the term 'boiled' is said to have been derived from this drink, as one of many synonyms for intoxication.

Every language prides itself on having the most twin words for 'drink' and 'drunk'. Miriam-Webster lists 177 for English, but the BBC once said it had a list of more than three thousand synonyms. Incredibly, it would appear that there is no drinking dictionary.

Wrong! Benjamin Franklin published his 'The Drinker's Dictionary' in the mid-18th century – as far as I know, the very first and last dictionary for drinkers. And 'boiled', which came later, is not in it.

Benjamin Franklin was one of the Founding Fathers of the United States. Along with Washington, Jefferson, Penn, and various others, he signed the Declaration of Independence.

We encountered him in school many years ago, but for a very different reason: he had a thing for electricity. Do you remember? He flew a kite during a violent thunderstorm and almost got electrocuted, but he still had enough breath to decide that lightning was simply made of electricity.

But he was much more! A politician, as we have just said, but also a mathematician, a meteorologist, a publisher, a writer and a gifted humourist. An anonymous source says that during the many, often tedious, discussions in preparation for the Declaration of Independence, he asked to speak only once: to ask if the window could be opened.

Between 1733 and 1758, under the pseudonym Richard Saunders, he published his annual 'Poor Richard's Almanack'. These beautifully illustrated books contained a calendar for the coming year, dates and times for the phases of the sun and moon, a horoscope, weather forecasts, puzzles, trivia, his own sayings, humorous articles and much more. 'Poor Richard's Almanack' sold like hotcakes.

In 1737, part of 'Poor Richard's Almanack' was reserved for 'The Drinker's Dictionary', announced with the one-liner: 'Nothing more like a Fool than a Drunken Man'.

In it, he lists no less than 228 (American) expressions for intoxication. Examples include 'His Head is Full of Bees' and 'Piss'd in the Brook', as well as many others. He is said to have jotted them down in pubs, insisting they were not borrowed from any other language.

Two hundred years later, the American journalist and writer Edmund Wilson added ninety-nine more expressions to the list, arranged according to degree of intoxication: from mildly intoxicated to criminally drunk. 'Boiled' was among them by that time, ranked in twentieth place.

Want to know what Wilson thought was the worst form? 'Burning with a low blue flame'.

I never saw that in Uncle Frans, and (it should be stated) his 'novena' never really lasted nine full days either.

People exaggerate easily.

Benjamin Franklin published his
`The Drinker's Dictionary' in
the mid-18th century - as far as I know,
the very first and last dictionary for drinkers.

9 Drinking Licence

The following scene occurred some 15 years ago, a long way from home.

I am chitchatting in the hotel bar with an American expatriate who knows all about the local distilleries. In between, we sip sparingly on a fine whisky. The barman follows our enjoyment with bright eyes.

"Highland Park 18 is good," he smiles.

Has he tried it himself? "No, sir, but this is a real one!"

He proudly displays a certificate of authenticity around the neck of the bottle.

It is a bottle with the old label design: no silver scrolls, Celtic twists, or Viking horns, just a black surface with gold lettering. Back then, content counted more than appearance. Highland Park 18 from that era was a gem. I don't think a Highland Park like this has ever been made since, even in Orkney.

> DRINKING LICENCE
> WHAT
> What a 'driving licence' is for driving a car, a 'drinking licence' is for buying alcohol.
> MAYBE
> An alternative to a new 'prohibition'

To be clear, I am not somewhere in the Highlands, nor anywhere in America or India, but in Muscat, the capital of Oman, a Muslim country.

Sultan Qaboos bin Said al Said even looked down benignly on my drinking from his ubiquitous photograph. 'His Majesty' – the phrase Omanis use to refer to their sultan – had died a few years before, but he would be remembered as the man who made Oman one of the most progressive and tolerant Islamic states. When he dethroned his father and took the throne in 1970, Oman had three primary schools, one six-bed hospital, ten kilometres of paved roads, little electricity, no newspapers... nothing. Wearing jeans was as taboo as drinking alcohol. Now you see women in modern outfits at the wheel of magnificent cars (the car must have been washed, otherwise a juicy fine will follow); Hindu temples, Catholic and Protestant churches, and the bar in your hotel generously stocked.

The Sultan had every reason to bring his country into the 21st century: Oman has a population of about five million, but more than 40 per cent are expatriates from Britain and other English-speaking countries. Mostly young men, leaving a huge shortage of marriageable women, but fortunately not of alcohol.

But Oman is and remains a Muslim country, and Muslims are not allowed to drink alcohol. According to legend, the Prophet introduced this rule after witnessing an argument between his followers. They had had too much to drink at a dinner in Medina, and one of them hit another on the head with a severed bone (the legend does not say what they had eaten, but it could hardly have been a wishbone). Result: no more alcohol.

But what do you do with the non-Muslims in that case?

The Sultan had probably read some history books (something leaders should all do) and knew that banning alcohol in the whole country was a guaranteed failure. He certainly knew what had happened in America with the 'noble experiment' of Prohibition: hundreds of thousands of jobs disappeared, the state lost $11 billion in tax revenue, hundreds of millions of dollars were spent on useless inspections... Crime rose by a quarter in the first year alone, and upstanding citizens became lawbreakers and smugglers. New gangsters got rich, and never before had so many people died from drinking dodgy liquor.

Qaboos introduced the 'liquor licence'. Expats can simply apply for such a licence. There are a few conditions: you must be non-Muslim, live in Oman, and have a permanent job. You can't spend more than 10 per cent of your monthly salary on alcohol. If you meet these and all the other conditions, you can have alcohol in your home.

But not on the street. If you buy some whisky from one of the few shops with an 'alcohol licence', you must go straight home. Your receipt will show the time of purchase, and if the police stop you, they will calculate (free of charge) the time you need to get home.

Tourists, however, can get all kinds of alcohol from the many licensed hotels and even buy a bottle at the airport, on condition they rush straight back to their hotel. Public drunkenness means jail and a fine; driving under the influence is pretty much suicide. Any violation of the alcohol law is punished severely. And it works. There is a peaceful atmosphere throughout Oman, and crime is very rare.

But there are distilleries in Oman!

Yes, of course, but they have nothing to do with alcohol. They mainly distil the resin of Boswellia sacra, the frankincense tree, into an essential oil that plays a vital role in medicine. The production process is certainly as fascinating as that of whisky, but the result is less delicious.

Oman has proved that a 'liquor licence' works. American campaigners have long dreamed of such a licence, even with points and a two-year trial period. In other countries, too, voices are being raised in favour of such a system.

This is perhaps an idea for a country like Belgium, where you can legally conceive a child at 14 but have to be 18 to taste whisky.

10 Bottled in Bond

In Europe, seeing the word 'whisky' on a bottle is a reassuring sign. We can be sure that the liquid in the bottle is truly whisky. This is guaranteed by EU Regulation 2019/787, which each Member State must implement faithfully as law. This legislation formally reiterates what the EU clearly stated back in 2008.

In a nutshell, 'whisky' or 'whiskey' (we are also allowed to use this second spelling in Europe) is a spirit drink made exclusively from a mash of malted grains, optionally supplemented by whole grains of unmalted cereals. These grains are first saccharified and then fermented. It is then distilled (but not more than 94.8% alcohol by volume). The distillate must be matured for at least three years in wooden barrels with a maximum capacity of 700 litres. The final distillate, to which only water and pure caramel may be added, must have colour, aroma and flavour derived from the production process. The alcohol by volume of the whisky must be at least 40% ABV.

The law is clear, and there are no loopholes.

BOTTLED IN BOND

WHAT

'Bottled in Bond' means that the whisky in the bottle meets several specific conditions

SYNONYMS

Bonded, Used in Bond, Aged in Bond

ORIGIN

In the United States, as a guarantee of authenticity for liquors

But in the past, the 'water of life' has not always been treated with the same consideration. Whisky and other popular drinks were often expertly mixed with the most lurid and toxic ingredients: arsenic, for example, was sometimes used liberally.

It was not until the Adulteration of Food, Drink and Drugs Act of 1872 that the maximum amount of arsenic that could be added to a cask of whisky was clearly defined. 'Moderation in all things' seemed to be the message. However, the culprit was not always the producer: since whisky was traded in casks, the contents sometimes underwent a 'slight modification' along the way.

It was not until around 1900 that people in the UK began to realise that something had gone wrong when hundreds of hefty drinkers suddenly died in central England.

Clever marketers are still all too happy (and rightly so) to put `BOTTLED IN BOND' in big letters on the label, sometimes `BIB' or just `BONDED'.

100
PROOF
STRAIGHT RYE
WHISKEY
ESTABLISHED 1810
BORN
in PA
MADE
in KY
OLD
OVERHOLT®
BOTTLED-IN-BOND
SINGLE DISTILLER / SINGLE SEASON / AGED 4 YEARS
STRAIGHT RYE WHISKEY
A Overholt Co
NON-CHILL FILTERED 50% ALC/VOL (100 PROOF)

In the USA, struggling with the same problem, an essential piece of legislation was introduced in 1897: the Bottled in Bond Act. The act aimed to protect the consumer and give the distiller a leg up.

Bottles that met specific conditions could now be labelled 'Bottled in Bond'. And those conditions were, and still are, uncompromising:

1. All the whisky in the bottle had to have been distilled in the same distillery, by the same distiller, using the same ingredients.
2. All the whisky in the bottle must have been distilled in the same season. There are two distilling seasons: spring and autumn, with January 1 and July 31 being the transition dates.
3. The whisky must be matured for at least four years in a wooden cask in contact with the wood.
4. The whisky must be bottled at 100° proof or 50% ABV (except for export).
5. Nothing other than water can be added to the whisky.

Hey, that sounds reassuring! At the time, this label was nothing more than a green stamp on the excise seal, but the stamp is no longer in use.

Clever marketers are still all too happy (and rightly so) to put 'BOTTLED IN BOND' in big letters on the label, sometimes 'BIB' or just 'BONDED'.

Savvy whisky lovers only need half a word.

And distillers are happy too: the law gives them a four-year reprieve from paying excise duty on their whisky.

The BIB applies not only to whisky but also to other distillates. Only vodka and gin have an exception to the five conditions: the wooden barrels in which gin and vodka are 'matured' must have a protective coating of paraffin or another substance inside to avoid direct contact between the alcohol and the wood.

As an ardent gin and vodka hater, I think this is genius: at least it cleverly prevents delicious aromas and flavours from entering your distillate.

BIB is not to be confused with 'Bag in Box': those cardboard boxes with a plastic bag inside that people use to 'bottle' wine.

11 D of T

D OF T

WHAT

Sometimes a letter is enough to indicate your self-identified label

WHAT IT MEANS

D stands for 'drunkard'
T stands for 'teetotaller'

WHERE

Mainly in English-speaking countries, but sometimes unexpectedly elsewhere

Suppose your great-great-grandfather saw you in a T-shirt that reads, "I'm not crazy. My mother had me tested." How would he feel?

He would probably complain that he ever extended the bloodline.

It may be understandable. But we need to understand that this is the new normal. The thing is, people don't have a problem with others wearing outrageous slogans on their clothes as long as it's a personal choice. The problem starts when it becomes mandatory.

D

In 1620, the legendary Pilgrim Fathers left England for the New World on the Mayflower. On board, they had plenty of water (which soon turned out to be undrinkable), but fortunately also had plenty of beer.

Beer was, therefore, the first 'civilised' drink that these pious pilgrims brought to New England (the north-eastern part of what later became the United States of America). But it would not remain their only 'comfort in difficult moments' for long. The French who followed brought cognac, which was also in demand, while rum was gradually imported from the Caribbean islands. It didn't stop there, either. By the early eighteenth century, New Englanders were producing their own rum – and a lot of it. Meanwhile, the heavy drinkers from the Low Countries (with their brandy and gin) had become Americans too. Then came a new culprit from Ireland and Scotland: whisky.

Alcohol was a gift from God, but the devil lurked around the corner.

Many settlers drank from dawn to dusk, if not to ward off the cold, then to sleep well. There was always a reason to reach for rum or other strong liquor.

Drunkenness became one of the biggest problems in the new society. Churches preached and preached against the pernicious stuff. The pulpit was an ideal place to get your message out to the crowd. Every church leader eagerly stepped up to point fingers at their imbibing neighbours.

Reverend Justin Edwards, born in Westhampton, Massachusetts, was descended from Alexander Edwards, who came to America from Wales. Edwards was a much sought-after speaker and well-known writer. He had his own views on drunks, as can be seen from a quote from one of his sermons: "Take the blood of a drunkard, from his head, or his liver, and distil it. You have alcohol. It has actually been taken from the brain, strong enough, on application of fire, to burn.

"Dr Kirk of Scotland dissected a man who died in a fit of intoxication. From the lateral ventricles of his brain he took a fluid distinctly sensible to the smell as whiskey. When he applied a candle to it, it instantly took fire and burnt blue."

But that did not always have much effect on drink consumption. The next step was stricter enforcement.

People caught repeatedly drunk were expelled from the church community. And the law became even severe. Those convicted of repeated drunkenness had to wear a large, bright red letter 'D' on their chest in public. 'D' for 'drunkard'.

'Woe to Drunkards. Two Sermons Testifying Against the Sin of Drunkenness', a pamphlet from 1712, teaches us that in those days, from all pulpits, a reproachful finger was pointed at the 'Dutch', referring to the Flemish and Dutch lumped together. Their ancestors, industrious workers (as you surely know), were the cause of all drunkenness and all the suffering that went with it, according to 'Woe to Drunkards'.

"There was a time, before the Dutch arrived, when a man could live seven years in New England without getting drunk. But what is it like now?" asks the preacher. This is clearly a rhetorical question.

The same sermon ends (thankfully) with redemptive words (at least if you fall into the right category): "An eminent clergyman from Holland, where this sin has been so prevalent for so long, explained that those who were great lovers of wine and strong beer suddenly saw what harm it did, so they repented and gave it up. But those bewitched by the love of brandy and other distillates can hardly be made to understand."

From then on, a red letter 'D' on the jacket meant 'drunkard'.

Once you have a great big 'D' on your jacket, go ahead and look for a job! We'll keep our fingers crossed.

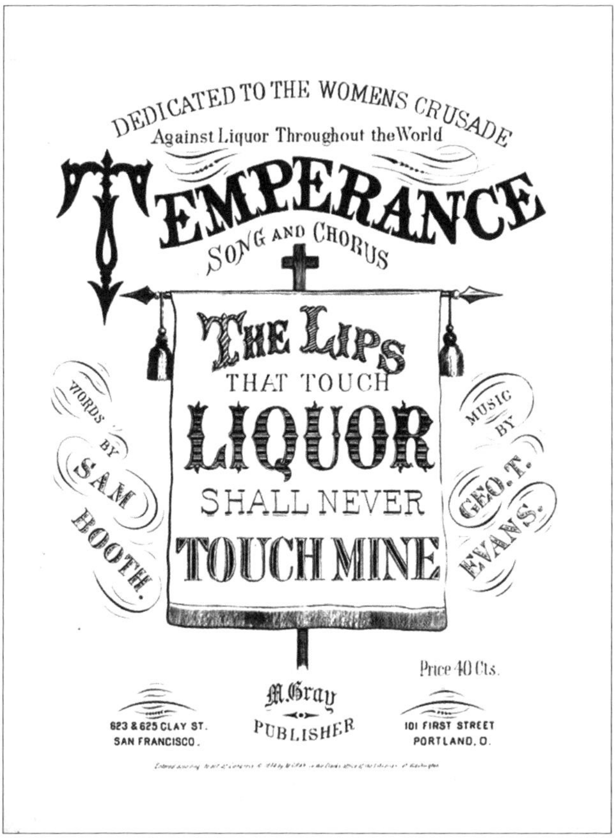

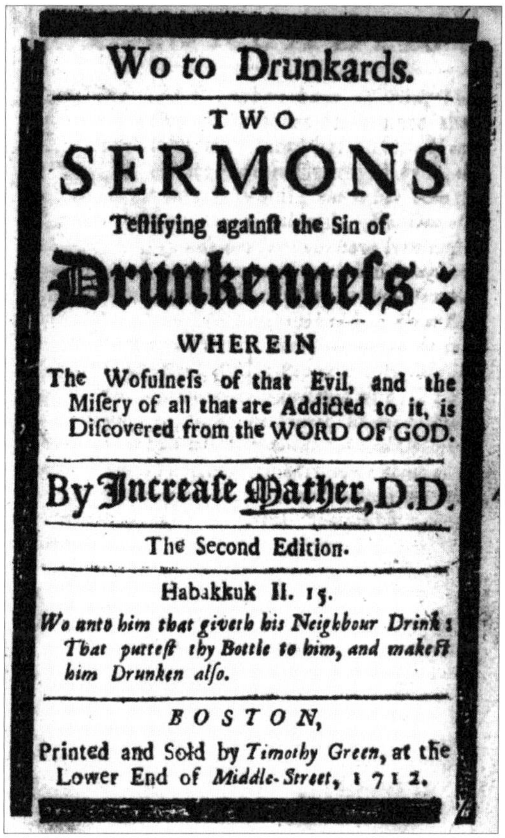
Wo to Drunkards.

TWO

SERMONS

Teſtifying againſt the Sin of

Drunkenneſs:

WHEREIN

The Wofulneſs of that Evil, and the Miſery of all that are Addicted to it, is Diſcovered from the WORD OF GOD.

By Increaſe Mather, D.D.

The Second Edition.

Habakkuk II. 15.

Wo unto him that giveth his Neighbour Drink; That putteſt thy Bottle to him, and makeſt him Drunken alſo.

BOSTON,

Printed and Sold by *Timothy Green*, at the Lower End of *Middle-Street*, 1712.

T

Around 1830, several groups emerged in England and the USA who were convinced that they had to point out the dangers of alcohol and urge people to give it up.

With tremendous success! Temperance halls sprang up, meeting places where people flocked to listen to these itinerant messengers of doom. People could sign papers swearing never to touch another drop. Lists were drawn up for people to confirm their decision. Members could choose between 'total abstinence' or 'moderation' (for those who still took the odd drink). Each member could indicate their preference on these membership lists: those who chose 'total abstinence' put a capital 'T' in brackets after their name.

Hence, 'T-totallers'. (The 'T' has nothing to do with tea.)

Famous teetotallers over the years have included Eric Clapton, Jennifer Lopez, Abraham Lincoln and Donald Trump (who has his own 'Trump Whisky', made in Scotland). Even Joe Biden shudders at the thought of alcohol, although the First Lady happily enjoys a nice glass of wine.

The Thomas Cook Temperance Hall in Leicester (UK) ↓

12 John Walker whisky

It was Christmas Eve 1492 when Christopher Columbus saw an island of green mountains in the distance. "You see, I was right!" he shouted. "This is Cipango!"

(We now call Cipango 'Japan', but Columbus couldn't have known that.) The Taino natives on the island laughed out loud when they heard the strange man in his crazy costume was convinced that he was in Asia. On board the Santa Maria, too, the crew were rolling around on deck, some from laughter, the rest from scurvy. In those days, it was hard to tell the difference between the two. In any case, it had been a long time since they had laughed so much in Quisqueya.

JOHN WALKER WHISKY

WATCH OUT

Not 'Johnnie', but 'John'

WHERE

Blended whisky which is hard to find

PRODUCER

Diageo

The natives called the island Quisqueya. Columbus called it Hispaniola after Spain, which came in handy: at least we would know who would doom the island in the coming years. The island is now divided between Haiti and the Dominican Republic.

Laughter would soon be lost on the Tainos. The Spaniards brought with them a plethora of unfamiliar bacteria and viruses. As a result, the Tainos contracted several diseases they had never heard of. This was good for their medical knowledge but not for their numbers; within a few years, they had dwindled from 400,000 to just a few thousand. The remaining Tainos vaguely remembered that memorable Christmas night but did not tell it to their grandchildren (or lack thereof), so we have to rely on Spanish historians for the rest of this historical record. And you know how reliable they are…

The Spaniards also brought along a few shoots of sugar cane, making Hispaniola the first island in the Caribbean to grow sugar cane. By 1516, sugar cane mills were already in operation on the island. The next step towards rum came naturally.

In the late 1970s, I wandered around there for almost three years, writing from island to island.

Tourism was still in its infancy, and hotels and restaurants were a rarity in many places. Scheduled island-hopping flights departed from small islands as soon as they could find someone to fly. For my flight from the Bahamas to Virgin Gorda, I was picked up at my hotel by… the pilot.

Everywhere you went, there was laughter, singing and dancing.

And rum was everywhere. At the bar of the Oloffson, a romantic Victorian hotel in Port au Prince, Haiti, where Graham Greene wrote 'The Comedians', the barman set me on the road to becoming a rum connoisseur.

More than 30 years later, my editor-in-chief sent me to Santo Domingo in the Dominican Republic for a week. After all these years, I have (by default) switched from rum to whisky.

In the meantime, the once-unknown island had also become a tourist attraction. You'd be hard-pressed to find another Belgian who wasn't lying there in the sun. In the all-inclusive hotels, the bars offer the most dubious drinks. Local rum is available as much as you like, but whisky only comes with unrecognised labels.

I found out that in Santa Domingo you could find a '*trago de etiqueta roja*' and a '*trago de etiqueta negra*' – red label and black label, as it were – and the occasional Ballantine's, but there must be more to discover.

A young lady in the Zona Colonial is trying to get me to warm up for a massage, '*masaje completo*'. She looks up in surprise when I tell her I'd rather enjoy a good whisky. Disillusioned, she refers me to Pat'e Polo, the oldest pub in North America. The Tourist Board should send more ladies like this down the lane!

During renovations in 1998, they found a threshold that refers to the pub's official opening in 1505. Its long history can be seen everywhere: in the shady interior, weathered walls, wooden ceilings, Taino carvings .... and servers dressed as pirates.

Pat'e Polo was the call sign of the mysterious Dutch pirate Johannes Frederikszoon. He had only one eye and was a cripple. That's why everyone called him 'wooden leg': Pat'e Leg.

You don't expect an avalanche of whiskies on a 'rum island', and it's truly surprising when you see a long row of them. When that happens, there is always a bottle that catches your eye. For me, it took no time at all.

Wait! Just a moment, is that truly a bottle of 'The John Walker'? Not 'Johnnie', but 'John'! I can't believe it! Probably another fake Johnnie Walker again! I've had some in Zimbabwe, China, India and South Africa.

But wait: the ornate case is covered in the same leather used for the Bentley, and the bottle is made of Baccarat crystal, lined with 24-carat gold.

You rarely see anything like this on counterfeit Johnnie Walker.

It has to be real. Let's check.

It was Christmas Eve 1492 when Christopher Columbus saw an island of green mountains in the distance. "You see, I was right!" he shouted. "This is Cipango!"

This whisky was launched by Diageo in 2010. They wanted to please John Walker, the founder who started it all. But considering the man left this vale of tears in 1857, they could never tell him first-hand. Only 330 bottles were made at that time. The blend comprises whiskies from nine distilleries that had been in operation in the 1800s when John was still alive. Some of these have been closed for some time, such as Cambus and Glen Albyn. The whisky is said to be beautifully balanced, fruity and creamy, with a hint of wood on the finish.

There are only 330 bottles, so get there fast – at least if you have the money, since a bottle will easily cost you a few thousand pounds. The whole of Australia, for example, had to make do with just ten bottles.

In the Caribbean, Pat'e Polo managed to get hold of one; it's perhaps the only one on the islands.

The bottle is opened, and you can taste it there.

Maybe next time, if my books sell well!

13 Christmas whisky

The town of Rochester, in the English county of Kent, has always been on the road from Dover to London. Most travellers now have to use a forced bypass, which is a shame because Rochester proper is beautiful and has a colourful history. Rochester Castle is a textbook example of what the Normans built there after 1066. The cathedral is also well worth a visit, and the quaint streets of the old town are a delight. But centuries ago, you really couldn't avoid it. Travellers just had to walk through it; that was the only route. For many, though, it was a welcome stop and a long-awaited chance for a hot bath and equally piping-hot food. But not for everyone.

CHRISTMAS WHISKY
WHERE
Rochester in Kent, England
WHAT
Whisky for 'poor travellers'
WITH A MORALITY LESSON?
Clearly

If you arrive on the High Street, in the shadow of the castle, keep an eye out for number 97. Otherwise you'll walk right past it, since the building has a nondescript façade, a door you must bend over to get through, and six colourless windows upstairs.

But this was once the place to be for a 'poor traveller'.

A stone plaque above the entrance makes it clear why this was a popular destination:

"RICHARD WATTS ESQ, BY HIS WILL DATED THE 22ND AUGUST 1579, FOUNDED THIS CHARITY FOR SIX POOR TRAVELLERS, WHO, NOT BEING ROGUES OR PROCTORS, MAY RECEIVE FREE FOR ONE NIGHT LODGING, ENTERTAINMENT AND FOUR PENCE EACH..."

Richard Watts was born in Rochester in 1513. When he died 66 years later, he had amassed a fortune and left a list of praiseworthy properties. In his will, he answered the call of his monarch, Queen Elizabeth I, who pointed out that rich people could use some of their wealth to fund hospitals, schools, hotels de Dieu and alms-houses.

Parliament went a step further and said that rich people should leave an annual sum in their will to alleviate the suffering of the poor.

Richard Watts had a brilliant idea; for years, he had seen strangers passing on their way to London without a penny for food or a bed for the night. In his will, he stipulated that a house should be fitted out so that six poor travellers could have their own bed in their own little room for a single night. They also had to be given something to eat in the evening and, at ten o'clock the following day, four pennies each in sound coin.

Richard Watts, who always added the word 'gentleman' to his name, had one condition: rogues and 'proctors' were excluded. The word 'proctor' was used to describe a specific type of beggar. Lepers, among others, were forbidden to beg in the streets. However, they could hire a 'stand-in' to replace them, a proctor. These proctors always had to be able to present proof of it, but it was even easier to forge proofs than it is now. Since it was impossible to keep track of the many fake proctors, it was safer to exclude them all.

Archetypum hunc dedit
JOS. BROOKE de SATIS Arm.
Sacred to the Memory
of RICHARD WATTS Esq;
a principal Benefactor to this City;
who departed this life Sept. 10. 1579. at
his Mansion-house on Bully-hill, call'd SATIS, (so named
by Q. ELIZABETH of glorious memory,) and lies
interr'd near this place, as by his Will doth plainly
appear. By which Will, dated Aug. 22. and proved Sep.
25. 1579 he founded an Almshouse for the relief of poor
people, and for the reception of six poor Travelers
every night, and for imploying the poor of this City.
The Mayor & Citizens of this City, in
testimony of their Gratitude & his Merit,
have erected this Monument, A.D. 1736.
RICHARD WATTS Esq; then Mayor.

But there was always a small problem: more than six candidates presented themselves almost every evening. Ultimately, it was the mayor's (or a deputy's) job to choose the six poorest. So everyone had to report to him at six o'clock. The lucky six were given a ticket and then had to go to 'the house', because the free communal dinner was served at seven: two hundred grams of meat, a sandwich and a cup of coffee. As they were only allowed to stay one night, there was no need for variety on the menu.

As this might have been too much for the mayor, he introduced the post of 'Poor Traveller Inspector' at the end of the nineteenth century. His job was to vet prospective sleepers thoroughly.

From the lists kept at the time, we know that these 'poor travellers' came not only from all over Europe but also from India, Australia and New Zealand.... In 1934, 355 years after its inception, a committee decided that an index adjustment was in order and raised the four pence to twelve.

Six years later, the Poor Travellers' House closed for good. The Second World War kept all the poor travellers away.

Once a year, on Christmas Eve, it was party time for the 'six poor travellers' who were lucky enough to stay at the house. On that day, there was always a wealthy citizen in town offering a whole Christmas dinner, including an aqua vitae! That evening, the six travellers dined in the house in the company of the benefactor and the mayor.

One of the benefactors was the writer Charles Dickens. In his wonderful short story, 'The Seven Poor Travellers,' he gives a colourful account of the whole event.

"Strictly speaking, there were only six 'poor' travellers," he begins, "but being a traveller myself, though an idle one, and being withal as poor as I hope to be, I brought the number up to seven. This word of explanation is due at once, for what says the inscription over the quaint old door?

'...for six poor travellers, who are neither rogues nor Proctors...'.

I know I am not a Proctor; I wonder whether I am a Rogue!"

Mr Dickens, good sir… Charles... listen... I know you advocate Prohibition... but believe me: someone who offers a stranger a whisky can never be all bad.

14 Bourbon

BOURBON

WHAT

A small county in the USA

BUT ALSO

The name of a typical American whiskey, said to have originated in the same county

CHARACTERISTIC

According to US law, bourbon whiskey is a distillate of a mash of malted barley and/or rye with at least 51 (but less than 90) per cent corn; aged in charred new oak barrels at 62.5% ABV

Daniel Boone in Kentucky.

Did you notice? This law doesn't mention Bourbon County at all. It's a crazy name, in other words. And it should be noted that Bourbon County no longer produces a single drop of whiskey.

It's a long story, and it all started with Daniel Boone. He was an eighteenth-century American adventurer best known for exploring what would become the state of Virginia. He literally paved the way for hundreds of thousands of fortune-seekers who fled Europe. These followers brought with them not only many customs but also various small stills. And they discovered an unknown non-European cereal in their new home: the kaleidoscopic 'flint corn' or 'Indian corn', a multicoloured variety of today's yellow maize. They called it 'corn'. Much to their delight, they discovered that their corn was very high in starch and would, therefore, produce a lot of alcohol. It didn't matter that the grain was very tough; they just boiled it.

And so Bourbon began in... Virginia. That state was absorbed by Kentucky in 1790. Originally, Bourbon County included thirty-four Virginia counties, but after the transition to statehood, Bourbon shrank to a tiny county, making it very different today from Bourbon County back then. During Prohibition in America, most of the distilleries disappeared from this county; by 1940, there was virtually nothing left. So, our bourbon whiskies are not made in Bourbon County but in Kentucky.

But not to worry. Others claim that the name 'bourbon whiskey' comes from Bourbon Street in New Orleans, where the new shipments of Kentucky whiskey originally arrived and were welcomed with open arms.

Others claim that the name 'bourbon whiskey' comes from Bourbon Street in New Orleans, where the new shipments of Kentucky whiskey originally arrived and were welcomed with open arms.

The cases were invariably stamped with the word 'Bourbon' in those typical stencil letters.

Either way, there's no need to dwell on it, because 'Bourbon' is not a protected regional name nor a protected product. There is no US law governing the name itself, but Congress did declare in a resolution half a century ago that bourbon is a "distinctive product of the United States". It's only 'American'.

What is striking is that it did not even refer to the state of Kentucky. Therefore, bourbon for the American market can be produced anywhere in the United States, even in Puerto Rico or Washington DC. But ... that is only the case for Americans, and does not extend outside the borders of the USA.

So YOU can make bourbon whiskey, and so can I – but not for the US market.

Look, in case you've already started making your own bourbon whiskey, wait a little longer (or keep quiet), because I've just discovered that in 2009, in order to please the Yankees, those friendly boys and girls in the European government decided that any bourbon whiskey or bourbon whiskey brought onto the table within the EU must also comply with US laws. When it comes to booze, they can play nice.

Finally, a word of advice: avoid getting caught by a bourbon biscuit; it doesn't contain even a drop of whiskey, let alone bourbon whiskey. This delicious biscuit is nothing more than two chocolate biscuits stuck together with chocolate cream. It's a delightful calorie bomb. It is easy to spot: there are ten holes in the top biscuit, neatly spaced in two rows, and in between are the words 'BOURBON' in big letters.

Why it is called 'bourbon' is anyone's guess. It was not made in Bourbon Coun-

ty or during the Bourbon dynasty. To add to the mystery, it was created by a German for a scone bakery in London.
The German's name was Hans Zehnloch. Get the joke? Zehnloch... German for 'ten holes'. Witty guys, those scone bakers. Forget it: those holes are just there to stop the biscuits from bursting during baking.

You probably don't care, because you're looking for a biscuit WITH whiskey in the first place. Just ask for a 'chocolate bacon biscuit with maple whiskey'. It has Jack Daniel's in it. But you'll also have to accept the crunchy bits of bacon (also one of the ingredients).

But I'll say this: you can blame it on my lousy character or my love of Scotland... but I doubt that the corn thing is American and not Scottish.

To the south-east of Edinburgh, you'll find the world-famous Rosslyn Chapel, built in 1440 (remember this date). The chapel is a magnificent piece of lacework made by gifted stonemasons.

All the windows have ornate border decoration, but there is one with... corncobs.

In 1440! Columbus was ten at the time.

And there was no mention of the Boone family.

Do you still believe this Bourbon story?

15 La Colonne Belge

You'll agree that whisky drinkers are down-to-earth people.

But now and then, after a sip of whisky, they can suddenly start spouting lyrical nonsense, laced with strange terms like 'oak notes' and 'leafy green smell' and even the occasional alliteration, as in 'sweet-salty-sea' flavour. These are tasting notes, and that in itself is harmless. But they become truly euphoric when they see those beautiful copper stills with their bulbous bellies and graceful necks. In these sacred places, the drink of the gods is born. Gorgeous, aren't they?

LA COLONNE BELGE

WHAT
Device for the continuous distillation of alcohol

INVENTOR
Irishman Aeneas Coffey?

OUR HYPOTHESIS
Before Coffey, a similar appliance had already been used in Belgium

But beware, boys and girls, appearances can be deceiving. Let's take a closer look at the distilling process. You pour a few thousand litres of wash into a still and heat the whole thing. That costs an arm and a leg. What do you get after hours of patiently waiting in that hot room? An alcohol of around 75% ABV, although technically, you can get 96.2% by distillation. True, at 75% your new spirit will also contain congeners, flavours, but at 96.2% it will not!

But two hundred years ago, when the Scots first exported their whisky to England, their southern neighbours didn't want those congeners. The rough drink was good enough for the rugged throats of those barbarians up there above the Tweed and Clyde.

To make gin, the English redistilled Scotch whisky to extract the alcohol and to remove the congeners.

In the early nineteenth century, inventors in several countries were looking for a device that would allow them to distil much faster, with much more alcohol, and preferably from the cheapest raw materials possible.

Although there were numerous inventors, all working independently, only two names usually appear in whisky books: Robert Stein and Aeneas Coffey. Stein was the first in 1829, but his method wasn't successful. The Irishman, Aeneas Coffey, did better. He was also in an excellent position to succeed: as Inspector General of the Irish Excise, he had access to many distilleries. He patented his revolution-

You'll agree that whisky drinkers are down-to-earth people.

ary distillation column in 1830. It was an instant success, except for the Irish, who were not happy with the technically tasteless alcohol that would soon change the market.

So, Coffey moved to England, and his revolutionary 'patent still' conquered the distilling world. The device was even named the 'Coffey still', and Aeneas Coffey is now universally known as 'the inventor of the automation of the distilling process'.

Well, there is a lot to be said of the latter.

It's not true!

In 1828, two years before Coffey's patent, the Dooms distillery on the Dender River in Lessen (Hainaut, Belgium) was already distilling with two columns. A year later, the Van Volxem distillery in Halle followed suit, and when Coffey was applying for his patent, the Claes distillery in Lembeek installed a new 'modern' column still.

The two Dooms brothers, sons of a Dutch industrialist, ran the largest distillery in the Netherlands, specialising in genever. Their columns worked according to the plans of the Frenchman Jean-Baptiste Cellier-Blumenthal, who moved to Koekelberg, near Brussels, around 1820. He got his inspiration from two other inventors – Jean-Édouard Adam and Isaac Bérard – and combined their findings. The 'secret' of these Belgian column stills spread quickly and aroused curiosity in other countries, including Scotland and Ireland. We know that Aeneas Coffey was very interested in the Cellier-Blumenthal still.

Not surprisingly, at Dooms, they managed to obtain 85% ABV. A record! Far higher than Stein or Coffey ever achieved.

In other words, the very first working alembic wasn't installed in Ireland or Scotland but in Belgium! It was called 'la colonne Belge' – in French, of course, the official language in the south of the country. We're not going to shout it from the rooftops, though. We prefer to let the Scots and Irish live in their illusions. They are sensitive souls.

Aeneas Coffey does deserve credit for refining Cellier-Blumenthal's plans to make the column even more suitable for heavy grain distillation, thus changing the entire whisky world. From 1860, the law allowed grain alcohol (from the column) and malt alcohol (from the pot still) to be mixed. This gave birth to the dominant (and often delicious) 'blended whiskies'.

So we owe the column to... Coffey? Cellier-Blumenthal?

No! If we have to thank one person, it's... Napoleon. Yes, the guy from Waterloo. Napoleon Bonaparte.

Not that the Emperor was actually trying to achieve modern whisky. He had other concerns: he had lost the Battle of Trafalgar in 1805 and wanted to punish the English. To that end, he banned all continental ports from receiving English ships and goods. That also meant he could no longer import cane sugar from the colonies. He had to switch to beet sugar, but refining sugar from beets required a lot of alcohol. So, he offered a prize of one million French francs (around eleven million pounds sterling today) to anyone who could develop an adequate continuous distillation system.

Unsurprisingly, Jean-Baptiste Cellier-Blumenthal, Jean-Édouard Adam and Isaac Bérard were all French.

And Aeneas Coffey may have been as well ; some historians claim he was born in Calais rather than in Ireland.

One of the 'sieves' in the old column ↓

16 Drinking whisky responsibly

Although I have always maintained that I would never reveal any of my secret recipes in my books, I am doing so now. You could call it a moment of weakness, but I am doing it because I could think of no better way to introduce this chapter. It also fits in well with my intrepid efforts to guide my readers towards responsible whisky drinking. Keep reading; you'll understand.

Take a piece of smoked eel out of its wrapper. About twenty-five centimetres long. To start, leave the fillet to 'breathe' on a plate for five minutes. (I know, eels don't breathe, but once it's smoked, it's different.) Take a full tablespoon of Talisker (any Talisker will do) and drip a whisky line where the late eel's bone used to be. Let the whisky slowly soak into the eel for about ten minutes. Stay with it to chase away any overeager insects. Meanwhile, toast thin slices of white bread very lightly. Sit down and enjoy. Note: you don't have to drink Talisker to enjoy this! Food pairing is the art of making food and drink work together during preparation but keeping them far apart in consumption. If you have three infused eel strips, your body will tell you that you need another Talisker after half an hour.

Then have a Talisker.

Because then you are drinking 'responsibly'. In this case, you are drinking 'with reason'. But that is not always obvious in many other circumstances!

By the way, it's high time we shed some light on these meaningless terms used in the whisky world! They beat you over the head with them these days: 'Please drink responsibly', for example. Do they mean, 'If you don't have a brain, keep your hands off our whiskies'?

DRINK WHISKY RESPONSIBLY

WHAT

Advertising term

MEANING

Not defined anywhere

IMPORTANT

Definitely

There are better ways to address your customers. And then this: 'We promote responsible drinking'. They pay thousands of pounds for a page in a magazine, hoping that as soon as you read it, you will put it down and run to a shop to buy a bottle. Come on, come on. Drinking responsibly? Has anyone ever told you exactly what that means?

Except me. And I want to go into more detail.

But it is simple. You only have to answer three questions to know if you are drinking responsibly: 1. Why are you drinking? 2. How are you drinking? 3. How do you feel after drinking?

To answer the first question, we turn to the unsurpassed French gastronome Jean Anthelme Brillat-Savarin. In his book 'The Essence of Taste', he answers clearly: we drink because we are thirsty. I know, Pliny the Elder once said: 'Man is the only creature that drinks even when he is not thirsty'! But Jean Anthelme disagrees. According to him, there is not one but three kinds of thirst: latent, artificial, and excessive.

A. Latent thirst

Latent thirst is the standard drink requirement because the body is losing fluid. This thirst allows us to drink at any time of the day. This thirst is a natural part of our lives.

B. Artificial thirst

Artificial thirst is an artificial pleasure rather than a natural need. This thirst cannot be wholly quenched because the drinks we consume always create a new thirst, unless we quench it with pure water.

C. Excessive thirst

Excessive thirst occurs when you have an increased need for fluid intake, and insufficient fluids are available. In the desert, for example.

OK, so far so good.

Option C does not apply, because we are not in a desert.

To answer questions 2 and 3, we'll fly to the other side of the world, to the National University of Hospitality and Tourism in Kaohsiung, Taiwan, the only hospitality and tourism university in the country. I first visited the university in 2008 and was quite impressed. The facility houses an extensive bar (featuring drinks from all over the world) and several practice areas: a pub, a chic boulevard cafe, a banquet hall, hotel rooms... and classrooms for about 4,500 students. Taiwanese whiskies were not available yet at that point (Kavalan only started in 2006), because whisky has only been allowed to be distilled in the country since 2001. But it was there that I was introduced to the art of Kaoliang Chiew and Sheohsing Chiew: Chinese fermented rice and wheat-based 'liquors' matured in ceramic vats.

Thanks to this knowledge (and further expert tasting), I have since learned how to use alcohol 'responsibly'. So it's true: not only the 'wise men', but all our knowledge comes from the East!

Now for the answer to question 2:

According to the Chinese, there are seven ways to drink alcohol.

1. Drinking alone
2. Drinking in pairs
3. Drinking in a group
4. Drinking exuberantly
5. Drinking shamelessly
6. Drinking without restraint
7. Drinking greedily

This is important because you can drink faster or slower in one category than in another. Note that you can fall into several categories at the same time.

And now on to question 3.

I discovered this in the East: the Chinese associate almost everything in this life with animals. There is nothing wrong with that. Which category did you belong to last night after the party?

1. Monkey-like: singing loudly, jumping around, reacting quickly

2: Lion-like: shouting, acting aggressive, macho behaviour

3: Pig: speaking unclearly and stammering when asking for another drink

4: Goat: shamelessly boastful but without a clear articulation

5: Wolf-like: become interested in the opposite sex and try to seduce them

6: Fox: pretending to be drunk and thinking they are fooling others

There are two other categories for which they couldn't find an animal:

7: Becoming sad, emotional and inconsolable

8: Passing out

Note: Again, you can mix several categories.

You see, those gentlemen in advertising have it easy with their 'drink responsibly'. As you can see, there are many things to consider; even the Chinese say so. But thanks to this chapter, you are now a lot better equipped.

Do you still have a question? Take a piece of paper and choose the correct category from the three answers above.

Then, make your decision: were you drinking responsibly or not?

If you are still unsure, you can show this list to your better half and hear what he or she thinks.

One more thing: those in uniform and hi-viz vests who sometimes stop you and ask you to take a breathalyser test probably still need to read this and may still have a somewhat outdated view of 'responsible drinking'.

Leave them to their wisdom.

So it's true: not only the 'wise men', but all our knowledgecomes from the East!

17 Whisky time

Fred Laing, the man behind the independent bottler Douglas Laing & Co and the planned Clutha Distillery in Glasgow, is a particularly friendly person. With his neatly trimmed and perfectly curled moustache, you quickly get the impression that he is always smiling and very happy. I would be too, I think, if I were sitting on a goldmine of sublime whiskies like he is.

One early and crisp autumn morning some years ago, we were expected at his home for a chat about our mutual hobby horse. As we had secretly hoped, he had five samples ready to go: five Port Ellens with ages that would make you shudder. One can't say no to that, of course.

As I said, it was very early in the morning, and his only regret was that we had already had breakfast. Not that he had also provided breakfast, but according to Fred, you have to taste whisky before breakfast. Only then is your mouth 100% ready to start serious work. After eggs and bacon, haggis, black pudding and beans, you can forget it. I'm inclined to believe him, because you'd have to look far to find someone with as much tasting experience as Fred Laing.

You wouldn't have to look far for another connoisseur to contradict him.

That one might say, "Eleven o'clock is the best time." And soon, another aficionado will stand up and claim that it's "nine o'clock in the evening, after a little rest."

Indeed, we could argue about this for a long time. Still, as you know, when I have thorny questions or other annoying problems, I always turn to my good friend and unsurpassed connoisseur Jean Anthelme Brillat-Savarin – but figuratively speaking these days, because the good man is dead.

WHISKY TIME

ASK YOURSELF

When is the best time to taste whisky?

ANSWER

I don't know that either

According to this friend, the French gastronome, it doesn't matter when or where you taste. It only depends on who you are: either you're a refined taster or you're not. And there's nothing you can do about it! What's more, your appearance reveals which category you belong to.

He supports this claim by quoting Johann Casper Lavater, a long-dead Swiss philosopher. Lavater specialised in 'human appearance'. From this and a person's demeanour, he could deduce what they were good at, what they had an aptitude for, etc.

Based on the theories of Lavater, whom he greatly admired, Brillat-Savarin deduced who was a gourmet and who was not.

So what follows is a way to discover at your next whisky tasting who will gain from it and who will be wasting his time. You don't necessarily have to tell them, however.

Brillat-Savarin states: "The male taster: not very tall, round or square face, rather a low forehead, small nose and round chin. The female taster: chubby, more handsome than beautiful, tending to gain weight, relatively short."

For the sake of completeness, he adds that in addition to the "born tasters" mentioned above, there are also "tasters by vocation". He divides these into four

I: Kobell Sculp.

JEAN GASPARD LAVATER

Citoyen de Zurich, et Miniſtre du St. Evangile.

Du Caractère humain profond observateur,
Chaque trait à ses yeux de l'Ame offre l'empreinte;
Et pour lui le visage est le tableau du coeur;
Où comme en un miroir la nature s'est peinte.
B:

groups: financiers, doctors, lawyers and clerics. Since I suspect that few of my readers fall into these categories, I won't go into that.

Should we now conclude with Brillat-Savarin that anyone not born a 'taster' can forget it for the rest of their life? And that there is no such thing as 'the best time to taste whisky'?

No: 'Whisky Time' does exist and is even internationally recognised! But Brillat-Savarin couldn't have known this, as he died in 1826.

'Whisky time' refers to a specific time of day. To please the Irish and Americans, we sometimes write it as 'whiskey time'. The term joins the ranks of phrases like 'Daddy time', 'Victor time', 'X-ray time', etc.

I must admit that this division of time is mainly used in aviation, shipping and the military. But nothing is stopping us from using it, too.

Here's the thing: the globe is divided into 24 zones, which we call 'time zones': that's how we know what time it is and why our trains always run on time. But military people, for some reason, call them 'military zones'. These zones all have names based on the NATO phonetic alphabet: Alpha, Beta, Charley, Delta... Please don't ask me why, but J for Julia is not used. Before 1956, the word 'William' was used for the 'W'. But as that was far too difficult to remember, they fortunately changed it to 'Whisky'.

Now we only need to know exactly when it is military 'Whisky Time'.

That's easy: Whisky Time is Coordinated Universal Time (CUT) minus ten hours. In other words, whisky time is Greenwich time minus eleven hours.

Always! No matter what time it is. And that's interesting.

Suppose you suddenly feel like having a whisky at nine o'clock in the morning. I said 'suppose'; I don't want to imply anything, but it happens. I've been there and can tell you what to expect: as soon as the whisky is poured, I'll bet your housemates will suddenly take you to task, while giving you an admonishing, questioning, disdainful look.

"Whisky? Already? At nine o'clock?" is the guaranteed cry.

Don't worry, you're on the right track: take out this book, turn to the chapter 'Whisky Time' and prove that it is, in fact, only ten o'clock at night, in 'Whisky Time'.

And nothing is to stop you from living in whisky time every day, starting with breakfast and switching to Coordinated Universal Time after your afternoon nap.

Believe me, it opens up possibilities.

18 Waterloo whisky

WATERLOO WHISKY

WHAT

Young Belgian whisky

FEATURE

Whisky with battlefield terroir

HOME BASE

La Ferme de Mont-Saint-Jean

I'm sorry; I hate history, too. But this time, I have to take you back in time: about two hundred years, but no more, I promise. 1815... that's doable, isn't it?

It's about a battle. What else did you expect?

On one side, Napoleon Bonaparte: a Frenchman. Nice guy, handsome fellow. Had great luck with the ladies. But walks around with the idiotic belief that he should own all of Europe. That wouldn't be so bad in itself, except that he has an army, and men with an army are always dangerous. That's one.

On the other side, Arthur Wellesley. Better known as the First Duke of Wellington, nicknamed the Iron Duke. Not an easy man, good strategist. Maintained friendly contact with William of Orange, King of the Netherlands and the Prussians. That's two.

Fortunately, Wellington did not know that those ugly green rubber boots would be named after him; otherwise, he might not have felt like making history. But he did.

On 18 June, 1815, Napoleon's and Wellington's troops faced each other at Waterloo. It was a short, fierce and bloody battle. With Prussian help, Wellington emerged victorious, and Napoleon was forced to abandon his dream of European conquest. Today, a lion stands forty metres towering over the battlefield, holding the globe under its paw. It looks defiantly towards France, the loser. In a nearby building, there is a beautiful (if slightly simplified) depiction of the battle. Unfortunately, the construction of this museum was granted to a company from... France.

La ferme de Mont-Saint-Jean ↓

Nearby, a farmstead named La Ferme de Mont-Saint-Jean stands on a large mound (behind which Wellington could hide part of his army and mislead the French).

The current building dates from 1719, but history books trace the farm back to 1219 when it belonged to the Hospitallers of St John of Jerusalem. Wellington decided to use the farm as the location for his battlefield hospital. Here, more than 6,500 soldiers (including wounded Frenchmen) were 'relieved' of a ruined arm or leg by a team of dozens of English and local surgeons. The interior doors of the farmhouse were converted into stretchers. Local women became 'nurses' and men became 'stretcher-bearers'. The courtyard of the farmhouse was littered with piles of amputated limbs: the result of operations without anaesthetic, unless you consider 'a hearty splash of the Scotch whisky and gin' to be anaesthetic.

'Nurses', 'stretcher-bearers' and 'surgeons' became the protagonists in the aftermath of the battle.

Edward Martin wanted to honour their memory in the whiskies he now distils at 'La Ferme de Mont-Saint-Jean': 'The Surgeon', 'The Nurse' and 'The Brancardier', the three firstborn Waterloo whiskies.

Edward Martin is the great-grandson of John Martin, an Englishman who moved to Antwerp in 1909 to import British and Irish beers. Martin's Pale Ale...

does that mean anything to you? Import was soon followed by the production of soft drinks, including Schweppes, in the Belgian town of Genval near Brussels. That Schweppes factory was later converted into the luxury hotel 'Château du Lac', a new step into the hotel business. Martin's Hotels currently owns 14 hotels in Belgium. Breweries followed naturally: Timmermans in Itterbeek, Bourgogne des Flandres in Bruges and the Waterloo brewery in 'La Ferme de Mont-Saint-Jean'.

It is at this farm that Edward Martin indulged himself to the full. He studied brewing and distilling at the venerable Heriot-Watt University in Edinburgh. Edward dreamed of setting up a distillery in Waterloo after his studies. But papa Martin was playing with the same idea, a pastime he wanted to reserve for his retirement. And you know how things go... So Edward was forced to wait patiently for dad to pass him the reins. Together, they started a small distillery with a tiny Ulrich Kothe still in the new wing of the farmhouse, where the Waterloo brewery and the headquarters of the whole Martin group are housed.

Inside the distillery, a spacious glass cage overlooking the battlefield, there is a tangible smell of malt and alcohol, but also the indefinable aroma of 'passion' as soon as Edward begins his story. Of course, you don't need to worry about your own wash with a brewery in the house. So, all Waterloo whiskies start with a (modified) beer recipe. Their blonde ale, 'Waterloo Récolte' in particular, is primarily used. Only their whisky 'Surgeon', a 54% ABV single malt, is made from the 'Waterloo Triple' beer. The 'Nurse' whisky is a 42% single cask grain, while 'The Brancardier' is a single grain.

Edward Martin: "With a 500 litre still, I can't produce in mass quantity. But I couldn't care less; I want quality made from local ingredients. Our barley grows on the battlefield. We create our products in the middle of an historical site. The Battle of Waterloo was a true turning point for our country and for Europe. I want to capture this terroir in my whisky and commemorate, in the names on my labels, the people who played a less conspicuous but indispensable role."

The casks sit in long rows in the maturation warehouse (where you can also see a surprising light show).

Edward Martin: "Until now, we used bourbon barrels and some new, uncharred French oak barrels. We recently decided to buy only French barrels in the future. I know the cask hugely influences the maturation of the whisky... but that is precisely what I want to avoid. These new casks give enough sweetness and taste of fruits and spices without overpowering the beer-wash aromas that I want to preserve!"

And what does this Waterloo taste like?

No, I'm not that easily tempted. Tasting notes are not my cup of tea. We are all old enough to discover them for ourselves.

Remember, 'the proof of the pudding is in the eating'.

But if I were you, I would surely do it. I have experienced it first-hand, and highly recommend it.

19 Nancy and the apple whisky

We would probably never have heard of Nancy had she gone through life as a good housewife. But that wasn't the case. Nor do we know her real name. History knows her as 'Nancy the Moonshiner', but that obviously wasn't her real name. We know that in the late nineteenth century, she lived in Warren County, almost on the border between New Jersey and Pennsylvania, near the Pequest River.

She was a strange woman who lived on her own, never socialising, minding her own business and leaving everyone else alone. She was sometimes seen picking fruit on the hillsides or hunting small game. She seemingly knew how to tan hides, which everyone thought was her main source of income.

When apples were regularly stolen from the orchards so abundant in the Pequest River region, the growers pointed the finger at Nancy's simple hut. This 'hut' looked more like a wooden stable leaning against the hillside. Although no one had ever been inside, it was easy to imagine that the interior would be far from luxurious.

Desperate, the apple farmers appealed to a detective, a man named Finch. He decided to keep an eye on Nancy's whereabouts. On the first evening, he hid in the bushes near the cottage.

Soon, a man carrying a heavy sack approached the cottage and entered without knocking. Finch waited for the man to come out, but no one reappeared.

NANCY AND THE APPLE WHISKY

WHO

Nancy the Moonshiner

WHAT

Moonshiner and bootlegger

WHERE

New Jersey

Thinking to himself, "Nancy is not as innocent as everyone supposes," Finch returned home that night feeling like a failure. He decided to start again early the following morning.

The first thing he noticed at the cabin the following daylight (day) was Nancy coming out and peacefully walking away.

Finch thought this was the perfect time to intervene. Finding the door unlocked, he carefully entered the hut and was stunned at what he saw.

Inside were a stove, a table and chair, a cupboard, and a few large baskets full of chestnuts. There were no apples in sight. A ladder led to an open mezzanine with her bed, a chair, and a barrel. Finch decided to hide there for a good view when Nancy returned.

It was already dark when she got home. She opened the door and used the moonlight to find her candle. Then, she lit the peat fire and climbed up the narrow ladder.

Finch watched as Nancy walked to the wall and pushed aside a wooden panel. The candlelight revealed the entrance to a tunnel leading into the mountain.

Nancy disappeared, reappearing a short time later... in men's clothing.

Finch bounded from his hiding place and pulled his gun; Nancy blew out the candle.

Only Finch could have put what happened next into words, but he didn't. We can hardly blame him, as he had received a massive blow to the head from a chair and was unconscious. And it was pitch black.

When people started asking questions the next few days, the police were sent to the hut. No trace of Finch or Nancy was ever found. The investigators discovered that a cave had been dug out at the end of the tunnel, and a small distillery had been built inside. Everything was there to make applejack, apple whisky. Even the (stolen) apples. And the business seemed to be flourishing, since there was a stock of more than 2,000 litres of ready-to-drink applejack.

It was also soon discovered what all those chestnuts were for: cover. Hidden at the bottom of the baskets were iron flasks which, after some puzzling, turned out to be perfect for tying precisely around the torso and legs and, when filled, were ideal transport during Prohibition.

Nancy was not only a moonshiner, but also a bootlegger. As it turned out, she was well-known and had clients as far away as New York.

But Nancy is no more, and neither is her applejack – although you can still find applejack on the whisky market.

I know, you're probably wondering how I came up with the idea of trying to make you believe that Nancy distilled in an enclosed cave carved into the side of a mountain, with no chimney or anything.

Calm down, calm down... That's not what I said.

She didn't DISTIL, she JACKED.

Jacking is another way of separating alcohol and water in a mixture. Distilling takes advantage of the fact that water and alcohol have different evaporation temperatures: the alcohol we want evaporates at a lower temperature than the water, so we can catch it in time.

Jacking takes advantage of the fact that water and alcohol have different freezing temperatures: the water freezes at a higher temperature than the alcohol.

Jacking takes advantage of the fact that water and alcohol have different freezing temperatures: the water freezes at a higher temperature than the alcohol.

So, what did Nancy do? With the apples she 'acquired', she made cider in the summer, with 8 to 10 per cent alcohol. During the harsh New Jersey winters, Nancy put her ciders outside. The water in her cider froze and the ice floated to the top, where she could remove it, increasing the alcohol in her kettle. What was left was her applejack, which now reached 40% ABV.

However, this method has one minor drawback!

We all know that when distilling, we leave out the 'head' and 'tail' and use only the 'middle cut'. When jacking, you cannot split the methanol and feints from the ethanol. And that is, to put it mildly, 'best avoided'.

So 'apple whisk(e)y', as it used to be called, is no longer on the market. Jacking is also no longer a common practice, and the applejack you find today is either a disguised calvados or a weak version of it, boosted with neutral alcohol.

And above all, beware of the many 'apple whiskies' coming from America.

These are whiskies made with apple extracts to taste like apples, even though no apples taste like whisky anywhere in the world.

Mind you, this isn't the only unsanctioned crime against the concept of whisky; there are others, and I guarantee there will be more to come.

20 Shebeen

You may know Wick, the small fishing port in the northeast of the Scottish Highlands. The city has a unique claim to fame: it has the shortest street in the world! Ebenezer Place measures just over two metres and has only one house and one door. Wick is the terminus of the train line that runs north, along the east coast, to Inverness. Heading out of Wick railway station and walking into town, you easily understand why some people call Wick 'the most desolate town in all the hemispheres'. Indeed, you wouldn't want to be caught dead there.

I've been in Wick several times, always in the rain. In fact, I wonder if the sun ever shines in Wick. But anyway, I love going there – because Wick is where my (Old) Pulteney is! It's incredible how one of my favourite whiskies was born and boosted up in a town that was dry until 1947.

In 1913, more than 65per cent of the residents voted to make the town alcohol-free. Pubs closed. Liquor shops closed. The Pulteney distillery was sold and resold and eventually closed in 1930. But Prohibition did not have much effect: in 1933, a Scottish newspaper block-lettered that, since Prohibition, more alcohol was being served in Wick than ever before. The editor stated: 'Wick has become one enormous shebeen.'

> SHEBEEN
>
> WHAT
>
> A dwelling where alcohol (primarily illegal) is served
>
> ORIGIN
>
> Shebeen is Anglo-Irish.
> In Irish: síbín
>
> APPLICATION
>
> The term was used in the entire (English-speaking) world but lost much of its original, often negative meaning and is now also used for legal drinking establishments

Shebeen?

Irish immigrants brought the concept and word 'shebeen' to Scotland. Wherever these Irishmen settled, informal drinking establishments known as shebeens emerged. As early as 1870, the 'North British Daily Mail' wrote that Glasgow had over two hundred brothels and more than one hundred and fifty shebeens. That these two institutions were mentioned in one go is not surprising. Shebeens were illegal bars or clubs, usually run by a woman (the Shebeen Queen), where whisky and beer were served (almost exclusively illegally) and where, in many cases, female 'beauty' was also present to relieve customers of any other urges.

The history books taught me very little about the actual charms of the 'beauties', but the drinks on offer were usually of dreadful quality, seemingly not shy of a dash of methanol.

The 'North British Daily Mail' divided the shebeens into two groups: the respectable and the non-respectable. The former merely broke the laws relating to excise, taxes, prostitution, and other purely worldly matters. In contrast, those odious, non-respectable shebeens were places where shady gatherings took place, conspiracies were forged, and gangsters held their meetings.

Understandably, these shebeens were a thorn in the government's side. Quite a few shebeen ladies and gentlemen (some owners were men) were regularly convicted, but the long arm of the law was no match for the masses. On the contrary, to avoid oppression, the government was cautious in drafting new laws.

In 1910, when the authorities wanted to bring the closing time for pubs back to 10 p.m., the case was abandoned for fear that even more shebeens would arise.

But it was not to last: by then, many countries had already taken up the fight against alcohol, and Scotland couldn't lag behind. The Temperance Movement also gained a foothold in Alba, and you can expect the unexpected from Scots.

In 1913, every Scot was allowed to choose whether their town would become alcohol-free. We know the story of Wick. Kilmacolm, located west of Glasgow, followed Wick's lead but refused to accept that pubs were allowed to reopen in 1947. Kilmacolm remained 'dry' until 1976, and it wasn't until 1998 that a new pub opened: The Pullman, housed in the 120-year-old station building.

But...

In the meantime, the shebeen had spread all over the world. You can find shebeens in the USA, Canada, the Caribbean, and other British crown territories, as well as in parts of the African continent, mainly in South Africa, where they gained a foothold during Apartheid. In the townships, they grew into temples of individuality and militancy.

The shebeens are still there, legally these days, with lots of booze, music and dancing. You can drink there, party with your friends, eat and even stay overnight. And if any other urges bubble up, some establishments offer solutions for that too.

You see, all's well that ends well.

Shebeen? Irish immigrants brought the concept and word `shebeen' to Scotland.

Wick Harbour during the Victorian Age. Readers with a keen eye will recognize herring barrels in the background.

21 Kosher whisky

It is hard to trace who first came up with the idea of 'kosher whisky' – commercially, at least. It must have been someone with a lot of market knowledge. There are about 15 million Jews in the world, a market not to be sneezed at.

Jews are allowed by their religion to drink a 'wee dram' in peace. At least if it is kosher: that is, if it complies with the rules of kashrut, the Jewish dietary laws.

It could well have been one of Lauder's people in Glasgow. In fact, Lauder's Blend is one of the oldest blends in the world. It was created by Archibald Lauder in 1834. The blend still exists today (now part of MacDuff International) and is instantly recognisable worldwide by its unique four-dent bottle. In the 1970s, there was a fierce advertising campaign with the likes of Yul Brynner and Dionne Warwick on the poster.

KOSHER WHISKY

WHAT

Whisky that fully complies with Jewish dietary laws

RECOGNISABLE

Usually identified by the ORT (Under Rabbinical Oversight) label on the bottle

Another advertisement for Lauder's Blend that appeared in Morocco around the same time is less well known, despite being fairly unique in the whisky world. The ad was undoubtedly aimed at the Jewish community, with text in four languages: French, Arabic, modern and medieval Hebrew, as well as in Hebrew script. It was all phrased in 'piyyut' form, characteristic of Jewish religious poems and songs that are often recited and sung at festivals, weddings and births. Where, of course, there was always whisky to drink. No one could doubt that Lauder's Blend was kosher.

As a Jew, you can only drink kosher whisky. This means that whatever is in your bottle conforms to the Jewish '613 Do's and Don'ts', particularly the section on food laws. These tell you what is allowed, what is not, and what is mandatory. In a nutshell, meat, milk, fish, eggs, and plant-based foods... are all permitted. But you are not allowed to mix meat and dairy products, for example, or to have them at the same meal. Also, any instruments used and the whole production process must not be contaminated by non-kosher elements.

For whisky, this is no problem. We use grain, yeast, enzymes and water, that's all. As long as we ensure that none of our ingredients come into contact with anything non-kosher. So, no worries… except for the casks where the whisky is to mature. And especially if you use wine casks. To be kosher, wine has to meet even stricter rules: among other things, people involved in its production must be practising Jews. However, such barrels can be found in the wine industry worldwide. So there are plenty of them.

The Milk & Honey Distillery in Tel Aviv is obviously on a roll. They are in contact with Jewish wine producers, and the bourbon barrels from the USA are all kosher. The late Jim Swan, a helping hand at the start of so many distilleries, made them put their whisky in the right casks and their 'Classic Single Malt Whisky', the world's first commercial Israeli single malt whisky, is a winner.

M&H
WHISKY DISTILLERY
CLASSIC
SINGLE MALT WHISKY
OUR CLASSIC SINGLE MALT WHISKY IS MADE USING THE FINEST EX-BOURBON CASKS AND OUR SPECIAL RED-WINE STR CASKS GIVING IT A LIGHT AND BALANCED CHARACTER MATURED UNDER THE TEL AVIVIAN SUN
TOMER L. GORIN
HEAD DISTILLER
700 ML
NON CHILL FILTERED
NATURAL COLORS
46% ALC/VOL

But they have another problem: Pesach.

Pesach, one of the most important Jewish festivals, is celebrated for several days every year in March and/or April, and is linked to several commandments. During Pesach, for example, a Jew cannot keep any fermented or soured foods made from grains such as barley. Therefore, Jewish whisky companies must sell their whisky stock every year before Pesach, or their whiskies will no longer be kosher.

So, how do you prove that your whisky is kosher?

Simple: you hire a couple of rabbis who will be happy to check things out thoroughly. A local rabbinate will appoint those responsible. In an emergency, you can also contact Rabbi Semelman Shlita, director of the Alcohol and Kosher Department of the Jerusalem Rabbinate.

If you plan to expand your whisky collection at home with an extra 'kosher' section, I recommend the KL&F website. KL&F stands for Kosher Liquor & Food.

The aforementioned Rabbi Semelman Shlita is also the director, so he should know. The website looks like a classic online shop, but nothing is for sale.

But not only whisky... they also list gin, brandy, tequila, rum... you name it, they can recommend a kosher option. Click through to 'whisky' and 'single malts', and you'll find twenty-five Scottish distilleries and all their kosher whiskies: neatly alphabetised, from Aberfeldy to Tullibardine.

It may be a mistake that the long-defunct rum 'Bacardi 151°' is listed among the Japanese kosher whiskies.

Still, at 75.5% ABV, it was undoubtedly kosher.

22 Mary Dowling

MARY DOWLING

WHO

Born in Kentucky to Irish parents

EXCEPTIONAL

Ran a large distillery in the early 20th century

AND

Founded the first commercial whisky distillery in Mexico

I have no idea who first said it aloud, but it will live forever: "The whisky world is a man's world!"

What nonsense! Like many things in our civilisation, we owe much of our whisky to the ladies. They rarely end up in whisky books, and if they do, then only as a 'nice anecdote' in a box with a coloured background and a snapshot of the lady in question.

What a shame.

For Scotland, they always bring up Elizabeth Cumming, who owned the Cardow distillery in Speyside in the late 19th century. Or Bessie Williamson, who ran Laphroaig in the last century. But remember: the list of ladies pulling the whisky strings in Scotland today or representing their whiskies around the world is getting very long.

Japan also has its leading lady, and a Scottish one at that: Rita Cowan. She married Masataka Taketsuru, who is at the root of Japan's entire whisky history. Masataka had a tough time getting out of the starting blocks. The Taketsuru household was on the verge of starvation, but Rita kept things on track, thus preserving the future of Japanese whisky.

The search is harder in the USA. That is not to say that women did not have any fingers in the pie; quite the opposite. It is estimated that more than 50 distilleries in the USA were owned by women in the 19th century, but we don't know which ones. You don't get much press if you don't have many rights. There are plenty of famous men, though.

Take Mr Jacob 'Jim' Beam. We all know him. But his wife, Mary Beam Meyers? Who's heard of her?

She not only gave him ten children (including sons who would later help him in the business) but also a hundred acres of land, inherited from her father, on which he could start a distillery. The fact that his ghost still roams in that distillery may indicate that he did not thank her enough.

Marge Samuels of Maker's Mark may be more familiar. She must not have been an easy lady. Her husband, Bill Samuels, bought the distillery in 1953, and a few years later, Marge summoned him to tell him she had a few minor criticisms: his whiskey was tasteless, the name wasn't right either and the label even less so. She redesigned everything herself, including the dripping red wax over the cork and the surprising slogan: 'It tastes expensive ... and it is'.

But one woman stands head and shoulders above the rest: Mary Dowling Murphy, referred to as the 'Queen of Bourbon' in the few books about her life.

Mary Murphy was born in Kentucky in 1858 to parents of Irish descent. She married John Dowling , a man twice her age, when she was just seventeen. They would have nine children.

John worked with his brother in a small distillery, which was taken over a few years later by two enthusiasts, M. Waterfill and G.G. Frazier. The company changed its name and became 'Waterfill & Frazier'. They were doing well, the distillery was growing, and Dowling saw an opportunity to buy in. He steadily

increased his shareholding and, by 1900, had taken over the whole business. He died two years later. Mary inherited the distillery and its management and immediately became one of the most influential women in the American whiskey world.

She quickly took control of all facets of the business, and its success continued. She became wealthy and was able to amass a considerable inventory of whisky in her warehouses. When Prohibition came in 1920, Mary changed her strategy. She sold half her inventory to other distillers who had a 'medicinal' licence, which she, as a woman, could not obtain.

She kept the rest of the whisky hidden under the floor of her house.

For four years, she was able to draw from this secret supply to sell to 'bootleggers' who supplied illegal bars and 'speakeasies'.

Until she was caught in 1924. Officers found more than 3,000 litres of whisky in her house. She claimed it had been there before Prohibition and was medicine for her and other sick family members, but that didn't fly. The whisky was confiscated, and she and her three sons were fined fifty thousand dollars, which is about three million today.

Mary decided she had had enough. Relocating the dismantled distillery, she and two of her seven sons moved to Juarez in Mexico, on the Rio Grande, just across the US border. She also hired Joseph Beam, a distiller and nephew of Jim Beam, to help her.

There, she established the Dowling Mexican Distillery, or D.M. Distillery for short: the first significant whisky distillery in the land of tequila and mescal. Its so-called 'bourbon whiskey' (it was actually a blended whiskey) was of the highest quality compared to what could still be found locally. In addition to the lucrative Mexican market, former clients in the US also stayed interested. Thirsty American tourists found solace in Juarez and took bottles home. But Mary had also discovered other channels to supply 'sick' Americans with medicine, mainly through the Rio Grande.

The D.M. Distillery became a thriving business, watched with envy by her American counterparts.

Mary died in 1930, four years before Prohibition ended.

While other (male) distillers in Kentucky closed their doors at the onset of Prohibition and sought another livelihood, Mary persevered, fought against national restrictions, and successfully overcame the obstacles.

Her sons returned to America in 1934 to resume whiskey production.

The brands 'Waterfill & Frazier' and 'D.M. Distillery' still exist today.

23 Bunnahabhain

BUNNAHABHAIN
WHAT
Whisky distillery on Islay in Scotland. Name of the accompanying malt whisky.
PRONUNCIATION
Bu-na-ha-ven (Scottish Gaelic)
MEANING
Mouth of the river

Would you do me a favour? It really won't take long! Just to see if, in the same situation, you have the same ideas I do. I'll keep it short. Listen: sit quietly with a bottle of Bunnahabhain in front of you. And watch intently... No, wait, I have a better idea.

Sit quietly, pour yourself a hefty golden dram of 'Bunnahabhain 12 years' and place the bottle in front of you with the label facing you. Enjoy the mild freshness of this beautiful island whisky. Notice the careful dosage of smoke (while its neighbours often burn peat like mad), nibble on the sweet maltiness and follow the valiant attempts of the fruit and floral aromas to gain the upper hand, and enjoy the suppleness with which the finish unfolds so slowly and lavishly.

Beautiful, isn't it?

I hope you have kept sight of the bottle, because that's where my problem lies. After the above experiment, and especially after a second and third whisky, I still feel that the word 'Bunnahabhain' contains a few letters too many. Do you agree?

You will understand that I repeated this test several times to investigate further.

Well, I have good news: this word has no excess letters at all! But there is something wrong with it. My Scottish Gaelic-speaking friend Alan was willing to investigate the matter thoroughly (provided I promised never to bother him with such idiotic questions again).

First of all: 'bun' does not mean 'mouth'; it means 'bottom'. Mouth would be 'beul'. But you'll agree that Beulnahabhain doesn't sound as good as Bunnahabhain. So, we agree with Bunnahabhain. But, as always, the devil is in the tail: 'abhain'. Look: River is 'abhainn' with 'nn' at the end. Why? The devil only knows. However, according to the arcane spelling rules of Scottish Gaelic, this word changes in certain expressions. And apparently 'mouth of the river' is simply: beul na h-aibhne. See the difference with the 'abhain' in Bunnahabhain? My friend Alan insists that the distillery is located in a part of Islay that has been uninhabited for centuries and was always called Bunnahabhain, hence the spelling on the bottle. We accept that, too. Agreed?

Now, the next point is that we have to pronounce that 'bh' as a 'v'. There's nothing Bunnahabhain can do about that. After all, the Gaelic alphabet only has 18 letters and 'v' is not one of them. Neither are w, x, y and a few others. But we'll get to that later.

So, we agree with Alan: there are no mistakes in Bunnahabhain (or any of the other whisky names written in this unpronounceable Gaelic). You should know this, too: Alan is 1.98 metres tall and throws tree trunks in his free time.

Sorry about all that, but now we can finally get started. Bunnahabhain was founded in 1881, one of several start-ups at that time, and with good reason.

Around 1860, blended whisky (a mixture of malt and grain alcohol) came on the market with overwhelming success. These blenders had more than enough grain alcohol, but craved malt whisky.

To build the new Bunnahabhain (and the associated houses), William Robertson enlisted the help of John MacDonald of Glasgow. Good decision: MacDonald was a renowned builder and patent holder for reinforced concrete. Bunnahabhain was the first distillery in Scotland to be built entirely of concrete.

The distillery has always been a maverick, and recently proved it again. Since 2022, a new extension provides all the steam the boilers need, where they burn the distillery's draft, woodchips, and other waste. This makes Bunnahabhain the first distillery to achieve zero waste from the production process.

Now, they only need to find a 'carbon zero' energy source – and they will achieve that shortly. In 2022, the Scottish Government gave the green light for 'Oran na Mara', Gaelic for 'Song of the Sea', an apt name for the ambitious project.

Nova Innovation, an Edinburgh-based marine energy company, will install underwater turbines in the Sound of Islay, the strait between Islay and Jura. This narrow passage between the two islands is famous for its powerful currents and surprising tidal effects. Nova Innovation has already developed a similar project between the islands of Yell and Unst in Shetland, where homes are now powered by tidal energy. Oran na Mara will provide carbon-free energy not only for Bunnahabhain but for all the other distilleries (and there are quite a few now) and homes on Islay.

This would be a significant success for Islay and for Scotland as a whole, which aims to reach carbon-zero by 2045.

It can only make the 12-year-old 'carbon zero' Bunnahabhain even tastier.

Sit quietly, pour yourself a hefty golden dram of `Bunnahabhain 12 years' and place the bottle in front of you with the label facing you.

24 The 'Whisky Watch'

The masterclass at the Glenfarclas distillery in Ballindalloch is an unforgettable experience. It's not just about the whiskies served, but also the surprising interior. The tasting room is actually made from a room of the old liner SS The Empress of Australia, which was salvaged when the ship was dismantled in a Fife shipyard.

When two men raided it in the early hours of Sunday, 15 May 2022, they did not come to admire the unique panelling, but disappeared four minutes later with twenty valuable bottles of 'family range' whisky, including a 60-year-old single malt. The haul was estimated at 150,000 pounds sterling.

Of course the building was equipped with CCTV, but the footage did not make the police any wiser. To this day, there is no trace of the bottles or the burglars.

THE WHISKY WATCH

QUESTION

What is the best way to survey maturing whisky?

RELATED QUESTION

Are modern cameras better than what we had in the past?

So you might ask, "Can't these CCTVs and all these other ingenious alarm systems be perfected so that we can prevent these robberies, or at least solve them afterwards?"

By stealing whisky, these gangsters have struck the hearts of millions of people around the world! Don't they understand that?

And how did they guard those vast treasures of whisky in the maturing warehouses before they had CCTV and all the other modern gizmos?

The answer is simple: with the help of our best friends... the animals.

And you probably immediately think of our faithful four-legged friend, the dog. Very logical but wrong.

Few distilleries have or have had a dog.

Ardbeg had one, known as Shortie. The dog in question was the neighbour's Jack Russell terrier. It would roam the distillery in the morning, enjoy attention and care there throughout the day, and then return home in the evening. Shortie was not a very reliable watchdog. Partly because he was no bigger than a sturdy shoebox, he could – at most – bite the ankle of a would-be intruder.

William Grant & Sons (Glenfiddich, The Balvenie...) employed two cocker spaniels: Toby and Kevin. But they were trained for an entirely different purpose: sniffing out bad casks in the warehouses. And they were champions at it. They would sniff the entire contents of the warehouses and pull out any casks that were going the wrong way. But you didn't have to ask them to keep an eye on things at night. You don't ask dogs with degrees to do that.

So, dogs as guards? No.

Cats, then?

Yes, many distilleries used to have cats. I say 'used to', because the 'Health and Safety at Work' and 'Modern Food Hygiene' regulations introduced years ago insisted that those cute examples of 'Felis silvestris catus' should be shown the door. No more catching mice, an age-old task for which they were irreplaceable. There are still a few distilleries with a cat running around, but they are usually so lazy that they pose no threat to 'modern food hygiene'.

In fact, Lindores Abbey Distillery has two cats: Vesper and Friar John Claw. Vesper, the calico cat, is naturally reserved and has it all perfectly sorted. After the first ray of sunlight, she effortlessly calculates where the warmest spot of the day will be and lies there until the sun sets. Brother John Claw, a black cat, is constantly in and around the visitor centre. He is always lying in a spot that everyone has to pass accepting the countless strokes and cuddles without opening his eyes.

You should also know they both starred in a Netflix documentary and are world-famous. Surely you'll understand that you can't ask a cat with such a track record to guard those stupid barrels.

Cats? No good either.

We could go through the entire catalogue of a zoo, perhaps hesitating at 'crocodile' or 'shark', only to end up with the one animal that has proven to be the ideal solution in the past: the goose.

If we had read our history books better in the past, we would not have had to search so far. In 386 BC, the Gallic Senones set out to sack the city of Rome. They made good progress until they reached the citadel. They sent out a scout at night to check things out first. The Romans were asleep, but the Senones did not know

that, inside the citadel, there was a flock of geese dedicated to the goddess Juno, the wife of Jupiter. And these geese were not asleep. Geese are light sleepers, if they sleep at all. Also, you should know that geese can gnaw, gurgle, honk, bark, cackle, whistle, and hiss (I looked it up).

I don't know the difference between one bird and another, but they do make a lot of noise at the slightest suspicious visitor, especially when they have eggs or chicks. Another thing is that, like many birds, geese can see UV light, which makes them fantastic watchdogs. Needless to say, it was not the best night for the Senone scout. The geese betrayed them.

Now you see why Ballantine's chose geese to guard their new maturing warehouse at Dumbuck, near Dumbarton, in 1959. Chinese geese!

Chinese geese are unpretentious, site-bound creatures that lay well, weed well, and are vigilant guards.

Ballantine's, now part of the Pernod Ricard group, is the second best-selling blended whisky in the world. They released their first blend in 1881. According to insiders, a Ballantine's would contain fifty malts and four grain whiskies.

Their first team of guards consisted of five geese and one gander. I can't help it, but 'gander' – it sounds ridiculous, and it is – is the correct word for a male goose. Whoever thought of that should be fired immediately. To console the gander, they called him 'Mr Ballantine's'. Within a few years, this team had grown to a flock of over a hundred geese. They did exceptionally well and caused a sensation, appearing on TV shows, making several press appearances and appearing in dozens of adverts.

Until fame rose to their heads, or was it the alcohol fumes they were constantly exposed to? Suddenly, it was revealed that the females were neglecting their eggs. They laid them but did not remember to hatch them. The eggs had to be incubated to keep the team going.

The solution was found in a dozen hatch hens; hatch hens like to sit on eggs and diligently fulfil their new job. Problem resolved.

Since that day, everyone at Ballantine's has been able to sleep peacefully. The Whisky Watch was on constant guard.

And life would have been endlessly rosy had not a few foxes settled in the area. Foxes don't hunt Englishmen (although the reverse is not true), but as the geese were Chinese, the foxes didn't see a problem.

With sadness, people at Ballantine's discovered that the famous 'Whisky Watch' team was gradually being thinned out. When only seven were left, the Ballantine's board decided to install CCTV and give the remaining guards a nice old-age pension in an animal sanctuary on the River Clyde. Much to their surprise, they met some veterans of the Whisky Watch who had not waited for the fox to bite their throats and escaped earlier.

So Chinese geese are the best watchers. They should have known that at Glenfarclas.

25 Playing with whisky

Some creatures walking the earth sometimes think life is nothing more than a game. These individuals are the architects of board games. You certainly know those time-wasters... Cluedo, Monopoly, you name it. Some of these guys think they can develop these toys themselves, create their own games, sail on this lucrative tide, and make a fat profit.

Ridiculous.

I am one of them.

As a maths teacher many years ago, I designed several board games that would happily guide my students, future players, through the wonderful world of axioms, theorems, algorithms and prime numbers. But I have also developed other games that did not require as much thought. And one day, I presented my new games to well-known game manufacturers at the Nuremberg Toy Fair. I was warmly received but did not have to show any of my models. I was given two minutes each to explain how each game was played.

PLAYING WITH WHISKY

WHAT
Whisky-themed board games

DISCOVERING
Usually, a whisky quiz in disguise

LOOKING FOR
A non-educational whisky game

I had never been back home so quickly.

After licking my wounds, I slowly repressed the memory of this youthful misstep and forgot the attempt and those bloody games altogether.

Until one day, some forty years later, I was suddenly presented with the 'Whisky Game'.

At that very moment, the words of that charming blonde lady from Ravensburger came back to me: "People who buy a game want to unpack it at home and start playing it five minutes later, not to unpack it and start studying."

In other words: 1. keep it simple and 2. don't be a teacher.

My 'Whisky Game', made in Canada, contains two boxes of small cards, each with a quiz question (there are one-point questions and two-point questions). The cards are nicely decorated with the tartan of the Scots Heritage Society (sic).

The rules take up barely half an A4 sheet (thus fulfilling condition 1: each player answers a question in turn, and whoever gets the most points wins.)

Overconfident, I reach for the 'two-point' pack.

I took the top card, which contained four questions, and chose one.

"Question 4: Which distillery is located near the source of St Drostan?"

I carefully repacked the 'Whisky Game' box and kept it in a cupboard for the day I needed to give a present to someone who once deceived me.

But it did revive my inner gamer. Afterwards, I scoured the internet for new whisky games. And there are quite a few. But on closer inspection, most of them boil down to the same thing: a whisky quiz in disguise, sometimes supplemented by a fairly superfluous board or cards of the "go back to START but don't pass the bank" variety.

Until I discovered The Whisky Game. Yes, I know it's confusing, but these games are all called 'The Whisky Game' for some reason.

But this Whisky Game was different.

First of all, it is a real board game: a relatively large board depicting Scotland and Ireland. A path winds through both countries, passing distilleries and pubs. You roll a die to see how many squares you can move along the route. You can even sail or fly between the two countries. So far, so good!

Only then do you notice the game's subtitle: "An educational fun board game for whisky lovers from all over the world." Damn... 'educational' too!

Then there are the inevitable cards, ten packs: six packs of question cards, one for each of the six regions into which the designers divided this small world of whisky, plus special cards, bottle cards, closed distilleries cards and person cards.

The latter feature ten icons of the whisky world, including Jim McEwan, Richard Paterson, David Steward, Billy Walker, etc. You have to choose one at the start, and it will help you throughout the rest of the game.

To cut a long story short, you earn points along the way, use them to buy bottles, and the one who ends with the most extensive collection wins.

The rules also mention that this is not a 'drinking game'. You don't have to drink whisky anywhere during the game.

Oof... that is reassuring!

Although I did take a dram to help me gain some clarity on the many different rules of the game.

Anyway, I continued wrestling with the pressing question: "Is there a non-educational whisky game?"

Yes, there is one: 'Bootleggers, the Board Game'.

Anything and everything that breaks the law or violates morality is in it. Forget what your parents ever taught you about honesty and charity, because you are about to play a starring role in a game set during Prohibition in America between 1920 and 1935.

You are a merciless money-grubber who wants to become a leader in the illegal liquor trade and, more importantly, make vast amounts of money. A little cheating and some shady alliances will help you control the market. You'll need quite a penchant for corruption, too. The aim is to make sure you get a foothold in the speakeasies so your lorries full of illegal booze end up where they need to be!

The game box is twice the size of any regular board game. It also comes packed with plastic attributes (140 in all: trucks, gang members, a cop, etc.), dice, lots and lots of money, a game board and... cards.

There are no quiz questions this time, but cards that can earn you money, among other things. The rules are so complex that it takes a few rounds to get the hang of it. But it boils down to this: you can steal from your opponents, sell to them, prevent them from delivering their whisky to certain venues, and so on. All of this can cost you some money, but there's plenty in circulation in that world.

Unless, of course, an opponent is targeting you and trying to get you out of the market, no matter how. And you can expect that even from your best friends.

Again, the directions state that this is not a drinking game, an excellent remark that may possibly save lives.

Experienced players will find it an engaging game with many possibilities, but most importantly, they will recommend that everyone stays sober until the end.

By all accounts, it is an ideal way to lose your best friends.

26 Uisge beatha

Henry II was the king of England in the second half of the 12th century.

Henry II was a Frenchman. No offence intended here; the English have rarely had an Englishman as king. In fact, in the more than a thousand years since 1066, the king of England has only been English for 169 years. The first, William the Conqueror, was French, and almost all of the following were French, Welsh, Scottish or German.

But Henry II could not have known. He used to *be quite well off:* not only was he the King of England, but he also 'owned' almost all of France. He was rarely home, so coins often depicted him on horseback: a genuine tourist, always on the move.

He was the first English king to visit Ireland in 1171, not out of curiosity but because the Irish were getting on his nerves. He didn't go alone either; nearly five thousand warriors accompanied him on 400 ships. He also brought the blessing of Pope Adrian IV, which wasn't necessary: when he arrived in Ireland, he didn't meet much resistance. He met a lot of 'Irish' who, like him, were descendants of Normans (or Flemish mercenaries), which made things a bit easier. The rest of this story would delve too far into the annals of history, but one small detail is significant.

The English, who were accustomed to a dull ale or a cloudy fruit wine at home, noticed that these 'half-savages' on the neighbouring island were drinking a relatively colourless drink for which they had a crazy, unpronounceable name: uisge beatha!

The English, always good at imitating sounds, conveniently condensed it to 'whisky'.

And the word was born! But 'uisge beatha' would also survive and find its way into every self-respecting whisky book. However, we don't know precisely how to spell it. In ancient writings, you'll see 'uisce', 'uisci', 'uisge', and a wide range of other varieties.

Samuel Johnson, the 'father of all dictionaries', wrote it as one word: 'usquebaugh' in his 1755 Dictionary, which is still regarded as a masterpiece of lexicography. The fact that Johnson was English, rarely drank alcohol, and had a low opinion of Scotland and the Scots (he once said, "You can make anything out of a Scotsman, but you must be able to catch him early enough!") does not change the fact that I am inclined to accept his spelling as the most logical.

However, it is much more annoying that no sources clearly stated how the drink was made. We only have a few travelogues that pay any attention to this. Martin says that in 1695, oats and barley were distilled on the islands, sometimes three or even four times. But that doesn't make us any wiser.

Shush now... don't worry, I have the answer!

And it's all thanks to an otherwise unknown G. Smith from Kendal in Westmorland. This G. Smith published a booklet in 1725 with the meaningful title: 'A Compleat Body of

UISGE BEATHA

WHAT

'Uisge beatha' is the cradle of our word 'whisky'

MEANING

Water of life

PRONUNCIATION

(W)isk'ke-baa-(ha)

THE QUESTION IS

Was uisge beatha really whisky?

Distilling, Etc'. The volume measures 15 by 18 centimetres and runs to just under 150 pages, but you can't imagine one single distillate that is not in it. Aniseed water, angelica water, cinnamon water, cloves water, mint water, lemon water... you name it. Not only do we get instructions on how to do it, but we also get a list of all the ingredients you need (along with the purchase price) and a reference price in case you want to sell this water of life (without taxes, of course).

What do we find on page 39? Tada... 'Fine Usquebauch': the answer to your and my question.

What do we need to start? Cloves, mace, nuts, cinnamon, coriander, ginger, pepper, liquorice, saffron, raisins, dates and sugar. The author also assumes that we have a small cask of molasses or some malt alcohol. And, of course, a small homemade still.

Could this blend indeed be the ancestor of our whisky? The source of our master nectar of the gods, our otherworldly ambrosia? Our water of life?

Fill your still with 30 litres of alcohol and add the cloves, mace, nuts, cinnamon, coriander, ginger, pepper and liquorice. Hang the saffron in a bag in the neck of your still. And fire away. Meanwhile, chop the raisins and dates, put them in an earthenware pot with alcohol, cover with paper and heat over a moderate fire for six hours. When it has cooled, pass it through a sieve, add sugar and finally, add it all to the new spirit from your still.

Leave the mixture in the barrel for eight days (add egg whites if it is too cloudy), and your 'Fine Usquebauch' is ready to be sold.

If you are interested, your ingredients cost 2 pounds, 17 shillings, and 1.5 pence (in 1725 prices). You can surely sell your barrel of Usquebauch for at least ten pounds!

You're speechless, aren't you?

Could this blend indeed be the ancestor of our whisky? The source of our master nectar of the gods, our otherworldly ambrosia? Our water of life?

I had, and still have, no reason not to believe this G. Smith.

Although... the name 'Smith' does not sound too serious.

In England, lovers renting a hotel room (and prefer that nobody knows who they are) register as 'Mr and Mrs Smith'. But that was probably not the practice in 1725.

By the way, in his preface, he writes: "... this being my first work, I hope it will prove acceptable to the candid and sincere reader. If anyone disagrees, I wish him to sit down and do better..." Sounds self-confident, doesn't it?

And yet, we are left with doubts.

Does 'whisky' really have anything to do with uisge beatha?

Will we ever find out?

A pressing question indeed, but I know my readers! As true whisky lovers, you don't want to dwell on it; you want to get on with it, and most of all, you want to know now: What did that G. Smith thing taste like?

Well, buy a bottle. Today, with some luck, you can buy a 'SwnY Mor', a 'whisky' from Wales.

In the 1970s, the Welsh Whisky Company released a blend of (Scotch) malt and grain whiskies, with the addition of spices. The latter was later not clearly stated on the label, and this misrepresentation (as well as a bit of tax fraud) led to the imprisonment of the three managers of The Welsh Whisky Company and the company's closure.

However, the bottles are still available.

And now it is time for some real whisky...

"Darling, where have you put my Old Pulteney? ...What did you say? Empty? It can't be."

27 Knickerbocker whisky

KNICKERBOCKER WHISKY

WHAT

Unique whisky from the Prohibition era in America

NAME

A knickerbocker is a trouser that ends just below the knee and tightens around the leg.

NOT TO BE CONFUSED...

... with 'plus fours', four inches longer – hence the name – and tied around the calf. Tintin originally wore a plus fours.

In 1809, a pamphlet entitled "A History of New Amsterdam" was published in the still-young United States, authored by Diedrich Knickerbocker. The readers quickly discovered it was not a boring history booklet but a fine satire on the Dutch in Manhattan. Knickerbocker was also clearly a pseudonym. The booklet's cover left no doubt; at the bottom, it said in small print, 'by Washington Irving'.

Irving was an American with Scottish roots; his father was from the Orkney Islands. Irving became famous for his many short stories, not least the Legend of Sleepy Hollow and its 'Headless Horseman', which still features in scary movies today. He was a witty storyteller and spoke several languages, including Dutch. Therefore, many of his stories dealt with the Dutch (and their traditions and manners) in New York and its environs.

'A History of New Amsterdam' initially received mixed reviews (which is always good for your reputation), but the author's pseudonym was to become even more famous! It quickly became the nickname of New Yorkers, and even the NYC basketball team proudly bears the title of the 'New York Knickerbockers'.

But there's more. Today, you can get Knickerbocker rum, Knickerbocker gin, Knickerbocker beer, Knickerbocker cocktails, etc.

And since 1928, even Knickerbocker whisky. Right in the middle of Prohibition. Of course, it was smuggled in from Canada and intended for New York and Boston connoisseurs.

The United States and Canada share the longest border in the world: 6,377 km. Imagine trying to guard such a terribly long border. Each checkpoint had to cover about 30 kilometres of border. Moreover, part of this border was defined by the course of the Detroit River: on one side the USA, on the other Canada. In 1928, during Prohibition, it was estimated that around 1,400,000 bottles crossed the river every month... one way, of course. Not surprisingly, eighty per cent of the whisky available in America was smuggled in from Canada.

A man in Canada who saw this coming had thoroughly prepared his own business: Samuel Bronfman, a man with Russian roots and a nose for money.

Mr Sam, as he was often called, entered the liquor trade and set up his own company, Distillers Corporation Limited, in Montreal. He bought and reopened a distillery and built his business into a vast empire, the likes of which we will rarely see again in the whisky world. In 1928, he acquired Joseph E. Seagram & Sons, a fairly large liquor company with no enthusiastic successors, and in one fell swoop, he came into possession of millions of litres of ready-to-drink whisky. He renamed both his companies 'Seagram'. He tried as best he could to circumvent the laws and offer his whiskies to his eager southern neighbours.

He even had good intentions! He wanted to give them 'pure' whisky, knowing all too well what dubious decoctions the Americans were drinking. It would make him a fortune.

On the 17th of January 1920, at precisely 12:00:01 a.m., the general prohibition in the USA began: 'The Noble Experiment', as it was very euphemistically called. But it quickly turned out not to be noble at all.

Rich people had already been able to stock up on alcohol, but most of the Americans suddenly found themselves without booze. Fortunately, Section 7 of the Act provided a solution: "…no one but a physician holding a permit to prescribe liquor shall issue any prescription for liquor."

Immediately, people identified symptoms of diseases that could only be treated with wine, rum or whisky. The clergy could also obtain wine for ceremonies and other needs in their local parishes. Vocations increased astonishingly. Alcohol smuggling immediately became a bottleneck profession, but the gangsters could quickly count on the exemplary citizen willing to bring the 'devil's drink' to the thirsty.

Crime rose by more than a quarter in a year. To identify possible violations, the government appointed 1,500 inspectors (out of a population of more than 106 million).

THE AUTHOR

Among other things, they discovered thousands of illegal distilleries, hundreds of hidden speakeasies where everything was available and, along with 'real whisky', incredibly unhealthy beverages were served.

The menu included cocktails with tempting names like 'sweet whisky' (containing e.g. sulphuric acid) or 'squirrel whisky', whose recipe remained a secret.

The most poisonous concoctions also circulated on the black market. Smuggled 'real' whisky was often contaminated and mixed to make more profit. Tests performed on confiscated bottles and flasks reveal what 'whisky' could contain: chloroform, petrol, iodine, mercury, ether, camphor, quinine, acetone, nicotine... to name but a few. It is said that more people died from drinking impure whisky during Prohibition in the United States than American soldiers killed in France during the Second World War.

Samuel Bronfman wanted to arm himself against this tinkering. His 'Knickerbocker Pure Rye Whiskey' was to become a 'must-have' in the USA, so he clearly stated on the bottle that his whisky was matured in wooden barrels and bottled by himself.

And he used a unique system: the tin box.

Each bottle was packaged in a box, similar to a can of corned beef or sardines. You could only open it with the ingenious key that came with it: a small iron rod with a slot at the bottom. Somewhere on the box was a tin tab that would fit into the slot, allowing you to roll up a metal strip and open the lid. So you could be one hundred per cent sure it was an authentic Knickerbocker. Not surprisingly, this whisky helped to build Samuel Bronfman's fortune.

Sure, you might have reservations about that. And you're right: smuggling is smuggling.

These days, you can apologise for past sins, and then all is forgiven.

However, Samuel can't offer an apology of his own, since he died in 1971.

We must remember that despite everything, Bronfman and his Seagram's, the most extensive drinks giant at the time, ran and changed the whole whisky world on that side of the ocean. And he also spent a lot of his capital assets on charity, schools and museums.

So what happened to Seagram?

In the 1990s, Seagram moved partly into the music and film industry. That new venture backfired.

Seagram crumbled, and parts of its drinks division ended up with Pernod-Ricard and Diageo, among others. And, as in the expanding universe, some of those assets spread further among the 'new' players in the drinks market.

But in the world of whisky, the Seagram name has become unforgettable.

28 Cashew 'whisky'

India is one of the world's largest producers of alcohol. Five of the top ten best-selling whiskies in the world come from that country. In the latest list, India occupies positions 1, 2, 3, 7 and 10. Of course, not all these whiskies are consumed within the country's borders. The country's legislation on alcohol is not the clearest in the world. India is made up of 28 states and eight union territories. Some of them prohibit the possession or consumption of alcohol, while others have rules that vary widely. The legal drinking age can range from 18 to 25. But there is one fixed rule: the legal blood alcohol limit is 30 mg. And alcohol fines are no laughing matter; penalties sometimes include years in jail.

CASHEW 'WHISKY'

WHAT
A poor man's whisky

WHERE
India, one of the world's largest producers of alcohol

NOTES
Fruity, nut flavour and a pungent aroma

Among the most lenient laws of the land are found in Goa, India's smallest state, located on the west coast. Goa is also home to the vast McDowell distillery, founded in 1898 by Scotsman Angus McDowell, where the crown jewel McDowell No 1 is distilled. McDowell No 1 is the world's best-selling whisky, with more than 700 million bottles sold yearly. Most of it is drunk within the country's own borders, but Africa, the Middle East, the United Arab Emirates and East Asia are generous buyers. There is no market for it in Europe because McDowell No 1 is not 'whisky' at all according to European law, since it also contains alcohol from sugar cane molasses.

But whisky is not the national drink of Goa. More than seven thousand small

Washbacks in India ↓

and large distilleries create their own whisky, which they call 'feni', locally pronounced as 'feniemmm'. By law, feni is a 'state liquor': it can only be distilled and drunk in Goa. Exporting it to other states in India, let alone to other countries, is strictly forbidden. Country liquor is cheap and plays the 'poor man's whisky' role.

Given the way feni is made, it could easily be called 'whisky' in the Indian sense of the word. As such, most producers do their best to sell an honest product, but you will always find individuals who tamper with the composition and peddle bottles that are best avoided – unless you enjoy drinking battery acid.

My first lesson in feni was at the Sahakari Spice Farm in Ponda.

A visit to the spice farm is highly recommended for anyone who, like any true whisky lover, is into spices, flavours and aromas.

Saadhanaa, the young lady who led us through the greenery, enthusiastically stopped to point out cinnamon, vanilla, cloves, cardamom, ginger, nutmeg, lemongrass and many other aromas and flavours, some of which we had never encountered in whisky before. (And which we wanted to remember to colour our future tasting notes).

She kept us on the spice trail for a while, but then suddenly turned down a small side road to take us to Pranab, the 'master distiller'. He was under the trees, diligently distilling 'feni'.

The so-called infrastructure of his distillery does not inspire confidence. There is a sharp, sweet-sour smell that is not really definable, but instead thought-provoking.

The base for Pranab's feni is the cashew apple. This false fruit looks more like a pear, with a kidney-shaped appendage (the natural fruit) at the bottom. Inside is the cashew nut we all know and love. The apple itself, which is seasonal, contains a lot of juice but can only be kept for a few days. So Pranab only distils during the cashew season: March and April.

He extracts the juice from the apples by crushing them in a hollow stone. He keeps the sweet and sour juice in an earthen pot in the ground for two or three days, where it immediately starts fermenting. His 'wash' is ready to be distilled. Illegal feni distillation is virtually impossible: the pungent smell that spreads from the process cheerfully betrays any ghost distiller.

In the 'bhann', a copper still cemented into a block of burnt earth, the wash is distilled for the first time. The result is a weak 'low wine' called 'arrack', barely above 10 per cent alcohol. This is followed by a second and third distillation, which takes about eight hours, with feni as a result. Controlling the pressure and temperature in the still requires a lot of experience and is regulated by the master distiller, who occasionally pours a bucket of water over it. He skilfully manages to conjure up about 25 litres of feni from 100 litres of wash. This pale yellow-coloured feni contains about 40 per cent alcohol.

Saadhanaa takes two glasses and pours a generous amount. A layer of foam immediately forms on top, which she tells us proves that it is a quality product. The word 'feni' is derived from this layer of foam.

We tasted it and, in complimentary (but honest) terms, noted the pleasant fruitiness and various nut flavours. But out of respect for Indian courtesy, we say nothing about the pungent, penetrating and far from tempting smell.

She smiles and points to her nose in understanding.

"Feniemmm... you love it, or you hate it," she says, unaware that she quotes an old Laphroaig slogan.

So you see how small the whisky world is: I am sitting in Goa, forty degrees in the shade, eight thousand kilometres away from Islay, thinking about Laphroaig.

Should she have access to this writing, my wife would object that I always think of Laphroaig, but I won't dwell on that now.

"Feniemmm... you love it, or you hate it," she says, unaware that she quotes an old Laphroaig slogan. The base for Pranab's feni is the cashew apple.

29 Women's protests and Burebista

At the beginning of the 20th century, an 'open letter' to all women was published in Hungary. The letter was signed by Stéphanie, Archduchess of Hungary and Crown Princess of Austria, Hungary, and Bohemia. She was joined by many noble ladies who added their names and titles to the pamphlet.

Their plea: "Hungarian women, help us! Women from all parts of the country, rich or poor, happy or unhappy, women of high or low status, help us. Alcohol has made so many of us cry! In fulfilling our duty to give a happy future to this country, to humanity and the unborn children, we women want to bequeath to the coming generations a morally purer and friendlier world. A world without alcohol! That is why we are asking for your help. We trust that there is not a single Hungarian woman who will not hear this."

WOMEN'S PROTESTS AND BUREBISTA

WHAT

The earliest mention of Prohibition

BY

Burebista of Dacia

WITHOUT

Female help

Stéphanie was the second daughter of Leopold II, King of the Belgians. She was married to Archduke Rudolf of Austria, son of Emperor Franz Joseph and Empress Elisabeth, better known as Sisi (thanks to Romy Schneider).

It was not the first time that ladies of high rank had become involved in alcohol matters, but Stéphanie of Belgium (as she is now known) was a woman of great stature. But she was neither the first nor the last woman to sound the alarm.

While learned gentlemen discussed it over a glass of wine, women were on the 'alcohol battlefield', both in Europe and America. Politicians were quick to recognise this temperance movement.

For example, at the first anti-alcohol congress in Paris in October 1903, the Belgian minister Emile Vandervelde took the floor. He is famous for the Vandervelde Law, which he introduced in Belgium in 1919 and was not amended until 1984. This law prohibited the sale of spirits with an alcohol content of more than 18 per cent in pubs and restaurants. Liquor stores could only sell spirits in quantities of at least two litres. A litre of gin then costs more than the day's wages of a common labourer.

Vandervelde specifically mentioned the women: "We have found strong allies in the wives of the workers." He said, "Women have become our most devoted propagandists. If their alcoholic husbands will not listen to us, in the long run, they will listen to their wives."

In America, too, it was mainly women who went to war. Six months before the start of Prohibition in the USA, the state of Ohio was completely free of alcohol. After all, Americans 'owed' it to the women of Ohio.

On 27 February 1874, after a speech by author Sarah Knowles Bolton, a procession of women dressed in black marched through the town of Berea: the Women's Crusade had begun. The women went from bar to bar, entered, knelt and began to pray and sing psalms aloud! Their weapon, the pray-in, clearly had an effect as the bars closed one after another.

The group of feisty women quickly grew into a full-blown movement, and saloon owners all over Ohio faced raids. This 'Ohio Women's Whiskey War' led to the formation of the Anti-Saloon League, which eventually led to Prohibition in 1919.

One crucial exception from history should be noted: Dacia's prohibition did not require women's help.

Dacia was a vast kingdom ruled by King Burebista, who lived from 82 to 44 BC. Dacia more or less coincided with where Romania and Moldavia are now.

Burebista was a wise and noble king who reconciled the many different tribes of the land. He was a man of authority, respected (and often feared) by the surrounding lands. He did not like the Romans, and Julius Caesar was far from his best friend.

Women's protest in Ohio ↓

WOMEN'S WHISKY WAR IN OHIO.—OPEN-AIR PRAYER-MEETING IN FRONT OF DOTZE'S SALOON, SPRINGFIELD, OHIO.—SKETCHED BY JOHN R. CHAPIN.

On the guidance of his advisor, the astronomer and philosopher Deceneus, Burebista introduced a "ban on wine and viticulture" around 50 BC. However, Dacia was a very fertile area, especially renowned for its excellent wines. It is no coincidence that Dionysus, the Greek god of wine and the counterpart of the Roman god Bacchus, was born here.

Historians say that the Dacian wines were of exceptional quality and were enjoyed by both men and women. Women also habitually sprinkled their clothes with wine for good luck. There was no evidence that their drinking led to debauchery or rioting, yet Burebista ordered the destruction of all the vineyards in the country. As far as I know, this is the first mention of a prohibition. After what we have seen above, it is understandable that he couldn't count on the help of the women.

But why did he do it? We found several theories.

The Romans are said to have attacked and seized one of his cities only because all his warriors were drunk. Others claim that neighbouring countries regularly invaded Dacia, causing much destruction, wanting to get to the vineyards and steal cuttings from the vines. We will never know.

One thing we do know: Burebista was murdered by his own people a few years later.

Prohibitionists can rarely count on sympathy from the general public.

Six months before the start of Prohibition in the USA, the state of Ohio was completely free of alcohol.

30 Forget 1495! Whisky is older

I love whisky books, especially because they always paint a nice picture of the history of our favourite drink. However, I get annoyed that they usually pretend it all started in Scotland in 1495 with Friar Cor in Lindores Abbey. Believe me, this is a great injustice to our water of life. The history of our whisky goes back much further!

Centuries further!

Join me on a journey back in time.

Hellanikos of Lesbos was a Greek historian born around five hundred BC.

He collected ancient legends and wrote a great deal about the history of his country and the world as it was known at the time. Unfortunately, only fragments of his writings have survived, but fortunately for us, one story will surprise us.

He wrote (loosely translated): "Wine was discovered in Egypt, and the Egyptians love it and drink a lot. But for those who could not afford wine, they made another drink with barley in the copper kettles of Dionysos. The people who drank it sang and danced for pleasure more wildly than the wine drinkers."

Look, as a whisky lover, you can't ignore that: barley... copper kettles... pleasure... dancing... What drink is he talking about? Obvious, no?

By the way, the philosopher and scientist Aristotle (born a hundred years later) copied Hellanikos's story and added: "Those who get drunk on wine always fall forward on their faces. Those who have drunk too much of this barley juice always fall backwards on their heads, for wine makes the head heavy, while the barley drink causes stupor."

These last words leave no doubt: he is not talking about a pint of beer but about whisky.

If you're still not entirely convinced, let's turn back the clock to the time of King Solomon, who lived a thousand years before Christ. Yes, the same Solomon you know for his wise judgment and his many, many gold mines.

King Solomon was very wise, although he never spent a single day at school.

In a dream, God allowed him to choose between two options. The first option was 'wisdom, wealth, and a long life', and the second was 'the death of all his enemies'.

FORGET 1495! WHISKY IS OLDER

WHAT

The first written mention of whisky is thought to date back to 1495

REACTION

Not true

EXTRA

We will solve another age-old dilemma

THE RECOVERY p. 273 'Sir, they kept me up.' He answered, 'No, *you* kept *them* up, you drunken dog.'

What would you do? He chose wisdom. It was a good choice, because he was already wealthy. He had built many temples, owned many mines, and had seven hundred wives and three hundred concubines.

So, judging by the latter, wisdom was unquestionably the only thing he lacked.

And it is thanks to his wisdom that Solomon is found in the Hebrew Bible, in the book of Proverbs.

This book starts by saying: "These are the proverbs of Solomon son of David, king of Israel, for acquiring wisdom and discipline, for understanding words of insight."

All the sayings are neatly numbered, and in Proverbs 31:6-7, we read:

"Give strong drink to the one who is perishing,
And wine to those in bitter distress.
Let beer be for those who are perishing,
wine for those who are in anguish!"

Did you see that? 'Strong drink' in 1000 BC, wow! I feel a bit sorry for Brother Cor and all his followers (see later under 'Aqua Vitae').

But I had to say it!

What would you have done if you had been in my place and found all this evidence? Credit where credit is due, as the saying goes. Right?

But I know you have something else to ask me!

"Is it true that too much wine makes you fall on your forehead, and too much whisky makes you fall on the back of your head?"

You see, this is a much more difficult question. First of all, you will find little testimony from people who have experienced it first-hand, since they usually don't remember the next day what happened to them. And if they do remember, you can bet they are not always reliable witnesses.

As you know, however, that can't stop us from digging deep for a sensible answer.

In 1782, James Boswell had to appear in court in the English city of Lancaster. Boswell was a Scot, a lawyer, a biographer (including the 'Life of Johnson', the greatest of all biographies), a womaniser and a heavy drinker. Colleagues had found him in the street, drunk and unconscious. A few days later, he received a letter to appear in court.

The charge against him, in Latin at the time, was: "Quare adhesit pavimento"... 'He stuck to the cobblestones'. Unfortunately, there is no record of the trial, so we do not know whether he was lying on his belly or on his back. Nor do we know what he had drunk, for Boswell was a man of more than one type of tipple.

It's a pity, but we are not discouraged.

We keep looking... and bingo!

Wigtown, a charming town nestled in the picturesque region of Dumfries and Galloway, is renowned for being home to the esteemed Bladnoch Distillery. It is also celebrated as 'Scotland's National Book Town', boasting an array of quaint bookshops that line its Bank and High Streets. It was amidst these literary havens that I stumbled upon an intriguing piece of possible evidence.

This event dates back to the sixteenth century. I don't know the exact year, but it doesn't matter. Dumfries was suffering from the plague. A local blacksmith, apparently called Tom, was a true Highlander, a hard worker, a great whisky drinker and one of the few unaffected by the plague.

"The devil sent us the black pestilence," he used to say. "If I ever get my hands on him!"

One evening, he had bought a bottle of the best whisky and was on his way home. Suddenly, the devil stood before him.

"You have mocked me," said the devil, "now you will pay."

To cut a long story short, they agreed to fight. It's a wrestling match... whoever's back is pinned to the ground first is the loser. If the devil wins, he gets Tom's soul; if Tom wins, the plague stops.

Tom takes a big swig from his bottle first, but so does the devil! Fair's fair. They take turns drinking. But Tom takes small sips, and the greedy devil drinks in big gulps.

You guessed it: before the fight has truly started, the devil staggers and falls over dead drunk.

Backwards! Lying down with his back on the ground.

Tom wins. Plague over.

The latter is less important to us... it's the 'backwards' that counts.

So now we know for sure: if you fall over from drinking whisky, you fall on your back.

That answers your question.

Happy?

What were you saying?

That still doesn't prove that wine drinkers fall on their faces.

Sorry, this isn't a wine book.

SEE

31 Triple distillation

The term 'distillation' is not the problem, but 'triple' is.

Distilling, that's obvious. We never think about it, but maybe we owe it to a moment of inattention on the part of the Creator when He tinkered together our globe. Or He did it on purpose: ethanol evaporates at a lower temperature than water. Water: 100°C, ethanol: 78.37°. It could also be that the Creator liked to work with a few decimal places. Anyway, our whole distilling process is based on this silly little fact: when you boil beer, the alcohol evaporates first, then the water. That way, you can divide things up neatly.

TRIPLE DISTILLATION

WHAT

Obtaining a 'new spirit' by three successive distillations instead of the classic two

PROBLEM

Sometimes, three equals only two and a half

Unfortunately, other types of alcohol evaporate before water, too. Methanol, for example, evaporates at 64.96°C, and propanol at 82°. Neither is suitable for consumption. Fortunately, the even heavier (and undesirable) alcohols evaporate at over 100°C.

When distilling, you have to fish out the toxic methanol as it evaporates and separate as much ethanol as possible, plus a bit of propanol (because there's some good stuff in there). This way, after two distillations, we are left with a drinkable 'new spirit' of around 72% ABV, a product with flavour of its own and capable of creating even more flavours and aromas.

"So why distil three times?" you rightly ask.

And you are right to add: "It costs money, takes time, and, to make matters worse, the third pass also breaks down some of the flavours."

"But you get a lighter, easier-to-drink whisky," I hear someone else exclaim, "and you have more copper contact, so fewer sulphur notes in your whisky."

Before we can stop you, you shout, "Yes... an easier-to-drink whisky? Isn't it because you get more than 80 per cent alcohol? Money, money, money!"

Stop it; we'll never get out of it like that.

However, the solution is simple: while everyone in the whisky world talks about 'triple distillation,' only a few actually distil three times. True, in Ireland, it seems like everyone sticks to 'triple'.

In Scotland, however, Auchentoshan, Springbank, and even the new Rosebank also do triple distillation. Even BenRiach has launched a triple-distilled. Mortlach, too! And while we're at it, even in Texas and Kentucky, some producers have ventured into triple distilling!

All is well and good, but the problem is that they do it in different ways. It often boils down to the same thing: one part is distilled three times and the rest only twice. It could therefore be said that triple distillation is actually 2.5 times distillation. Someone, apparently with a lot of spare time on his hands, has calculated that Mortlach scores higher. The distillery has six stills, divided into three groups of two. They split the promising liquid in different proportions between the three groups during the production process. This way, the new whisky would be distilled 2.81 times.

Voilà, we can live with that.

In some distilleries, the process is different.

But in many cases, it still comes down to this: the wash goes into the wash still, and the 'low wines' are divided into two parts: strong and weak. The strong ones go straight to the third distillation, while the weak ones are distilled again in a second still. Of these new low wines, we only keep the strong ones, and they also go to the third still. This way, the strongest low wines are grouped. They are distilled together again, and at the end, the master distiller splits the head, heart and tail.

Auchentoshan is a textbook example of a true triple distillation. They also use three stills: the wash still, an intermediate still and the spirit still. The wash goes into the wash still at 8% ABV. This way they get low wines of about 27% ABV. These low wines go into the intermediate still (along with the 'tails' from the previous distillation) and are re-distilled. The result is what we conveniently call 'low wines' again. Of these, we only keep the middle cut, the strongest part. The rest we take back to the next second distillation. These strong low wines now go into the spirit still and are distilled a third time. From this we keep only the middle cut, while the rest goes back to the next third distillation. So, some are distilled three times, others four.

But for the dram I've just poured, I don't care if it's distilled twice or three times... as long as it tastes fine.

32 The I'm Alone incident

On 25 March 1929, the Canadian newspaper 'The Halifax Herald' devoted an entire front page to the good ship I'm Alone. The reason why was given in three lines across the width of the paper: 'Feelings Running High over Sinking of I'm Alone' followed by 'JUSTIFIES SINKING OF SCHOONER' and finally 'Trouble for United States Is Now Forecast'.

The Herald was only one of many newspapers that cleared its front page for the big news. And it was not only Canadian publications that picked it up, either; it was obviously big news in the USA, too, and even the French and British found it more than worth mentioning.

The I'm Alone must have been an extraordinary ship.

The I'm Alone was a forty-metre-long schooner with two 100-hp diesel engines and an experienced captain: John Thomas Randell. Captain John was a seasoned veteran who had proven his skills in both the Boer War and the First World War, and he knew how to get the most out of his fast schooner. The I'm Alone was registered in Lunenburg, Nova Scotia, and the ship sailed under the Canadian flag.

But the I'm Alone was a thorn in the side of the US Coast Guard! They had been chasing it for more than six years. They knew all too well that the ship made regular trips to Belize (part of the British Commonwealth), each time carrying back rum, brandy and whisky! The boat would then quietly return to the USA, bobbing in the ocean just outside the territorial waters, until small smuggling ships came to pick up the precious cargo and sneak it into America, during its Prohibition era.

The Coast Guard almost caught the schooner a few times, but John always managed to escape. In fact, John had a significant advantage: he knew the code the Coast Guard used to encrypt their messages and had a radio allowing him to eavesdrop on the Coast Guard's transmitter. As a result, the I'm Alone usually knew in advance when they were being chased. Whenever John realised he was being followed, he would steer his schooner out to the open sea at high speed to ensure he was out of US territorial waters.

But that was precisely the problem that arose in March 1929. At that time, it was internationally accepted that territorial waters extended 12 nautical miles from the coastline. But the Americans themselves made an exception: if it was a smuggling ship, the US Coast Guard could intervene as far from the shore as a boat could travel in an hour! Of course, this was a very flexible concept: with a swift ship, it could well be more than twenty nautical miles!

On 20 March 1929, the I'm Alone was sighted in the Gulf of Mexico, a few miles off the coast of Louisiana. It was the Walcott, a slightly slower Coast Guard vessel, that

THE I'M ALONE INCIDENT

WHAT

The US Coast Guard sank the Canadian schooner I'm Alone

WHY

It was a smuggling vessel

WHEN

1929, during Prohibition

had the dubious good fortune to encounter Randell and his crew. The Americans ordered the I'm Alone to stop, but the captain disagreed and sailed on into the Gulf. Once safely out of US jurisdiction, the two captains struck up a conversation, but Randell refused to surrender the ship.

Meanwhile, the Walcott had already received reinforcements from a second Coast Guard ship, the Dexter. The frustrated captain immediately ordered the I'm Alone to surrender. The schooner remained under fire for half an hour before disappearing beneath the waves, battered and bruised. One of the crew could not be saved: Leon Mainguy, a native of St Pierre et Miquelon, a small archipelago south of Newfoundland and part of the French Overseas Territories. Randell and seven others were captured and then imprisoned in New Orleans. Randell stated that the I'm Alone had been more than two hundred miles from shore, so the Americans had no right to attack the ship. The British government bailed them out, and the crew was released.

What followed was a back-and-forth between Canada, the US, Britain, and France. They all had a stake in the incident. Canada and Britain argued that it was an 'act of war', while France stuck to 'piracy'. Canada kept a low profile at first, as more than half of its industry ran on American investments. Nevertheless, the Canadians demanded some $400,000 for the damages they had suffered. But the Americans were not having any of it.

By chance, they had discovered that the I'm Alone wasn't Canadian at all, but actually belonged to a certain John Magnus, a Boston gangster who made his fortune smuggling liquor. Magnus had once refused to be part of the criminal 'union' known as The Big Seven (the 'alcohol mafia' under which other gangsters worked) and operated independently, hence the name of his schooner: the I'm Alone. The Yankees also discovered that the US bootleggers paid Captain Randell and his crew monthly and had even paid for Leon Mainguy's coffin.

The dispute between the four nations dragged on until 1935. Finally, an international commission of inquiry decided that the US government was at fault and had to issue an official apology to Canada. They were also slapped with a bunch of fines: 25,000 dollars to Canada, 10,000 dollars to Mainguy's widow and 25,000 dollars to the crew of the I'm Alone. Randell took 7,900, and the crew members split the rest.

That was where the story ended, but the I'm Alone wreck remains. Next time you go diving in the Gulf of Mexico, look around! Somewhere on the bottom are 35,000 bottles of whisky, rum and brandy: the cargo of the I'm Alone. You can't miss it.

All those bottles are centenarians!

33 Black and White

You would have to be from another (whisky-less) planet not to think of those two cute little dogs, Scottie and Westie, when you hear the words 'Black and White'. They have been featured on the Black and White Whisky label for over a century: a slightly overconfident (black) Scottish terrier and a somewhat shy little sweetheart, the West Highland White Terrier. It would take a lot of work to find a more explicit reference to the name of this whisky.

But the question (like the chicken and the egg) is: which came first, the name or the two little dogs?

BLACK AND WHITE

WHAT?

The brand name of a Scottish blended whisky

BLENDERS

James Buchanan

NAME REGISTERED

In 1904

The Canadian-born Scot James Buchanan blended his first whisky in the late 19th century. He packaged it in all-black bottles with a white label with black lettering. However, there was no 'real' brand name on the label. It simply said 'Buchanan Blend Scotch Whisky'. It's not a hit, I admit. Something like that doesn't sound very tempting. In the bars, customers would ask for "one of those black and white ones." It slowly became a nickname: "Black and White." James Buchanan was clever enough to see that it could make money. He patented the name in 1904, and all the ads immediately got a new look. The familiar black-and-white bottle had to give way to beautiful black-and-white drawings of chic ladies and gentlemen, or street scenes that would not have looked out of place in Dickens's books. But even this theme quickly changed, with horses and black-and-white dogs of various breeds appearing.

Even a Canadian sledge dog was given a place of honour on the label in 1910. It had supposedly been the only dog to survive Ernest Shackleton's legendary South Pole expedition. The truth is that Shackleton took 99 dogs and a cat named Mrs Chippy with him to Antarctica. According to experts, three dogs survived the expedition: Oscar, Gunner and Towser. After being rescued from the ice, they went to Wellington Zoo in New Zealand. Anyway, the fake husky in the ad would soon have to make way for a more domesticated scene. In 1912, James Buchanan himself launched a clever idea (which he'd had in mind for a long time): the inseparable Scottie and Westie.

They first graced an advertisement over a century ago, and are still 'walking strong' today.

No other pair of dogs has ever starred together in so many blockbuster films and with so many celebrities. James Bond grabbed a Black and White in several films, and Marcello Mastroianni, Cary Grant, Dean Martin, and many others did the same. Even the Tarzan films were affected (although Tarzan himself was a teetotaller). Walt Disney himself, it seems, did not go to bed without his Black and White.

And then there is the Englishman Herbert Kilpin, founder and first captain of AC Milan. It is said that before every game, he would hide a bottle of Black and White in a hole behind the goal in case he had to concede a goal. A sip always eased the pain, he claimed.

He died at the age of 46, according to the experts, from "excessive consumption of alcohol and cigarettes."

Proof that smoking is unhealthy.

34 Crown Royal Whisky

When Elisabeth Bowes-Lyon, the future Queen Mother, visited Canada with her husband King George VI in 1939, she was given a bottle of Crown Royal Whisky. She must have liked it very much: on the return journey, she had one hundred and twenty of these bottles in her luggage.

Elizabeth, Queen Consort Elizabeth, I should say, lived, as I am sure you know, to be one hundred and one.

She always claimed she owed her longevity to one single habit: drinking a large glass of raw milk every morning. Not skimmed milk, which had been sterilised of anything harmful, but milk 'straight from the cow'.

CROWN ROYAL WHISKY

WHAT?

World-renowned Canadian whisky

STRIKING

A maverick in advertising

She did not mention that she also drank a gin and Dubonnet in the morning, a lot of wine at lunch, then port, several martinis in the afternoon and champagne at dinner. Obviously, she was not a whisky drinker.

Was she a heavy drinker? According to the recommendations later issued by the government presided over by her daughter, Queen Elizabeth II, she was well over the "recommended amount of 21 units per week." She would be at 70 to 80 units. But let's not focus on that!

She must have been impressed by the Canadian whisky she was given.

Crown Royal Whisky was a ten-year-old blended whisky. It was made using a secret recipe from no less than fifty carefully selected whiskies. The bottle, with a gold-plated stopper and a label full of gold lettering, stood on an impressive base in the shape of a royal crown. "Delicately smooth and creamy with a hint of oak and the sweet taste of vanilla," it read. The whole thing was neatly packaged in a purple pouch sewn with gold thread. Samuel Bronfman, who acquired Seagram ten years earlier, signed off on the creation.

The name, the bottle, the purple bag, and the excellent blends would make them famous around the world.

Crown Royal Whisky was initially only sold in Canada. It

Crown Royal Whisky was initially only sold in Canada. It would be 1960 before the blend was available in the United States.

would be 1960 before the blend was available in the United States. Today, this 'whisky fit for a king' is the best-selling Canadian whisky in the world. But its launch in the USA had its problems. After Prohibition in 1933, many rules severely restricting alcohol advertising were introduced: no advertising on radio or television, no dates of or references to events taking place on Sundays, no pictures of women, no phrases such as 'bonded', 'bottled in bond' or anything similar, no promises, no comparisons, no references to soldiers in service or on missions, etc., and especially no messages directed at women.

This is strictly enforced by the Alcohol and Tobacco Tax and Trade Bureau, among others, but also by the Distilled Spirits Council of the United States. The Distilled Spirits Council is one of three trade associations specialising in the noble art of lobbying and, of course, the fight against alcohol abuse. Among other things, the council compiled a code of conduct for the entire spirits industry and tried to soften the sharp edges of the new laws.

These rules were relaxed in the 1990s. However, all the TV networks agreed not to broadcast alcohol ads, and the National Football League (NFL) also held firm that there would be no publicity for alcohol surrounding their sport.

But, as my grandfather used to say, even the devil will dance for a bag of money. In 2017, the first commercial during a football match was for... Crown Royal, with a clear message aimed at... the ladies.

And they didn't stop there.

'Kick Off with Crown Royal' added an eye-catching twist to the Super Bowl, the final between the champions of the two football leagues, capping off a year-long charity campaign.

Together with well-known sports reporter Erin Andrews, they selected the 56 most influential women in the US sports world. Each was presented with a bottle of Crown Royal 18, and for each, a thousand dollars was added to the million-dollar fund that supports institutions and associations that want to be part of the annual Super Bowl celebration.

And so it was, slipping in through the back door, that they entered the once-forbidden world of sport and the world of women simultaneously.

That left only the armed forces.

Crown Royal launched an original promotion in 2010 that is still going strong: the Purple Bag Project. They ask customers to return the iconic velvet purple bag in which their newly purchased bottle was packaged. Each returned bag, along with one dollar, was sent to 'Packages from Home', an organisation dedicated to assembling and sending care packages to military personnel stationed worldwide.

Meanwhile, Diageo (which now owns Crown Royal) sent more than a million 'purple care bags' to US troops worldwide through 'Packages from Home'.

In terms of branding, this operation has been more fruitful than a 'generous' golf tournament at St Andrews or Gleneagles.

35 What is 'The Whisky Case'

In 1878, a pamphlet with the all-telling title 'Truths About Whisky' was published in Great Britain. The tiny work, less than 100 pages, included four full-page illustrations of Dublin distilleries: John Jameson and Son, Wm. Jameson and Co, John Power and Son, and George Roe and Co. These are also the publishers of the booklet. They get straight to the point on the first page and say what is on their minds...

WHAT IS 'THE WHISKY CASE'

WHAT

One of the most important pieces of legislation in the history of whisky

WHEN

Late 19th, early 20th century

PROBLEM

Can alcohol distilled in a column still be called 'whisky'?

I summarise: "The four whisky distilleries by whom this book is published have for the past two years been engaged to place some check upon the practices of the fraudulent traders who sell under the name of 'whisky' alcohol from the column still (what they call 'silent spirit'), variously disguised and flavoured... This fraudulent trade... exists mainly thanks to the retailer; for if he would insist on getting whisky when he asks for it, and only 'silent spirit' when he asks for it, there would be an end to the fraud which is now so common."

To understand these men's anger, we need to briefly reflect on the years before that. Until 1830, all whisky was distilled in pot stills, those ornate copper stills to which every whisky lover respectfully bows his head. The raw material was always malted barley. This system is elaborate, slow, and expensive, but it produces a 'new spirit' of about 70 per cent alcohol, with flavour.

In 1830, Coffey patented his column still (although he is not its inventor... see under 'Cambus'). This system can hardly be called graceful. But it is fast and produces a 'silent spirit' of around 90 per cent alcohol, albeit without flavour. What's more, any agricultural product that can be fermented can be used as a raw material in this process. It was quick and cheap.

The Scots loved it immediately and eagerly installed the new column. Most Irish people spit on the floor with disdain at the idea: "That stuff is not whisky."

In 'Truths About Whisky', they once again put their finger on the problem:

"... Damaged grain and potatoes, waste molasses and various other waste products are thrown into the all-consuming maw of the patent still, and they all yield alcohol and water, nothing else... In fact, these things don't make whisky any more than they make wine or beer."

To make matters worse for the Irish, it was legislated in 1865 that it was allowed to mix these two types of alcohol (which had previously been impossible due to different tax rates). The result: blended whiskies hit the market. A huge success. The blenders (a disgusting species, according to the Irish) made a killing. And the Irish, most of whom did not own column stills, stood by and watched.

You will have noticed that these Irish distillers have used 'whisky' without an 'e' in this article, even though three of the four signatories to the pamphlet were already releasing their whiskies as 'whiskey'. But they had a good reason for dropping the 'e': 'Truths About Whisky' was not aimed at the Irish market but at the Scottish distillers, especially those using the new column stills, and at the blenders, for whom the book's authors had little respect:

"And say that there are still people alive who seriously believe that blending good and bad whisky is a desirable practice in the interests of the consumer."

Several large grain distillers that already formed the DCL, the Distillers Company Limited (see also Cambus) took up the fight against the Irish grumblers.

JJ&S

TRADE MARK.

John Jameson & Son,

Bow Street Distillery, Dublin.

J

TRADE MARK.

Wm. Jameson & Co.,

Marrowbone Lane Distillery, Dublin.

P

TRADE MARK.

John Power & Son,

John's Lane Distillery, Dublin.

GR

TRADE MARK.

George Roe & Co.,

Thomas Street Distillery, Dublin.

The Scottish pot still distillers were not sleeping on the job either. In 1903, when the London borough of Islington condemned two blenders for using the word 'whisky' in their blends, it looked as if the pot stills would win the case.

With a limited budget of £4,000 and the grain whisky Combus as its flagship, DCL successfully launched an advertising campaign in favour of 'single grain' whisky.

Finally, in 1908, the government set up the Royal Commission on Whisky and Other Potable Spirits to resolve the matter. After 37 hearings and a year later, the verdict followed: distillates from pot stills, column stills, and mixtures of the two could all bear the word 'whisky'.

An outstanding victory for column users and especially for the blenders.

Had it been the other way around, today's whisky world would be very different.

36 Aqua vitae

This simple sentence from the Scottish Exchequer Rolls of 1494 should be in every whisky book: "To Brother John Cor, by order of the King, to make aqua vitae: VIII bolls of malt."

The 'King' is James IV; 'Brother John Cor' is the brewing and distilling brother at Lindores Abbey in Newburgh; 'VIII bolls of malt' would make about 200 litres of aqua vitae.

Obvious, right? According to the Scots, this is the oldest written reference to whisky.

But wait a minute.

Johann de Cuba and Johann Boil were both physicians working for the city of Frankfurt in Germany. Together, they wrote a pamphlet warning: "The drinking of aqua vitae is strongly discouraged for children, pregnant women and the elderly with weak health."

In 1484. Ten years before John Cor and his 'eight bolls'.

And the message is much clearer, too: read that sentence from the Rolls carefully. There is no mention of this aqua vitae being sent to James IV. Perhaps it was a gift from the king to the monk, and the latter could do with it as he pleased. A gift for services rendered. John Cor was also often found in the king's company. Not that we doubt James's orientation, mind you. In fact, he was married three times. The first time was when he was one year old. His bride, Cecily Plantagenet, was older, though she was five.

But OK, the aqua vitae had to go to James. That doesn't mean he drank the aqua vitae – on the contrary.

AQUA VITAE

WHAT

Latin for 'water of life'

IMPORTANCE

Regarded as the first written mention of 'whisky'

TRANSLATION

Gaelic: uisce beatha; French: eau de vie; English: water of life

Thanks to Pedro de Ayala, a Spanish diplomat at James's court, we know a lot about the king, including that he and the people at the court ate a lot but drank very little. Perhaps this aqua vitae was meant for something else. It could also have been used as a medicine, a disinfectant, to make gunpowder, etc.

James was well-versed in all these practices. He was not the prettiest man alive, but he was clever. He spoke nine languages (including Flemish), studied architecture, and, above all, medicine. Teeth-pulling and bloodletting were just two of his unusual skills.

So we don't know, but we have to go on.

Anyway, I am inclined to conclude that the story of the German doctors about aqua vitae is older than that of John Cor. My friends Helen and Drew, owners of Lindores Abbey Distillery, may not be happy to read this, but it is the truth.

So, let's forget Cor and give the honour of the first mention to the two Johanns. At least we know that their aqua vitae was only for drinking.

Just a quick note: in her book 'Water of Life', Anne Wilson says that in 1415, the Benedictine monks of Durham Abbey in northern England entered in their accounts the cost of buying and repairing stills (clearly marked) 'for the production of aqua vitae'. In 1415! That means our evidence for the German doctors is slightly weak. Did we decide too early?

Not at all, because in 1387, King Charles of Navarre groaned with pain in his arms and legs. To alleviate his suffering, he was wrapped in cloths soaked in aqua vitae and neatly sewn up by a diligent maid. She can only be blamed for using a candle to burn through the thread. The cloth caught fire, and the king died. This clearly proves that this aqua vitae had a high alcohol content and was older than Durham's.

And so, for a while, we can travel back in time to the furthest reaches of the world as it was known then.

But have you noticed that the Irish are absent from this story?

Logically, we therefore need to go back deeper in the timeline. Yes, we know, for example, that Lord Coke highly recommends 'uskebach' to Lord Coventry: "to drink Irish uskebach every morning, it will help to drive away all frightful thoughts, dispel winds, and keep his insides warm all day long." But that was in 1622. We have better!

The Red Book of Ossory is one of the most important medieval Irish manuscripts. It was written by Richard Ledrede, the Bishop of Ossory, around 1348 when the plague broke out in Ireland. It contains 60 hymns and other texts related to the faith. But it is particularly prized for its three and a half pages in Tironian shorthand, which was used mainly in monasteries. In it, the writer gives a detailed account of the medical use of aqua vitae. This is irrefutable proof that the Irish knew how to use whisky long before the Scots. This would be the oldest reference anywhere.

That means we're done.

Except for the following, of course.

There are no mentions of what they used to distil. Was it barley?

It was probably wine. A Spanish visitor wrote in his diary that the local wine was distilled in some abbeys because it was distasteful otherwise. The same probably happened in Durham. And also by those two Germans... Branntwein. And also with Charles of Navarre.

Only Brother Cor clearly says 'VIII bolls of malt', i.e. malted grains.

Conclusion: the 1494 entry is indeed the first to define whisky.

Happy now, Helen? Drew?

37 Peak whisky

Cactus Island, of which Whiskey Peak is the capital, is a small island in the East Blue Sea known to avid computer game players. The island is owned by a somewhat obscure group called 'Baroque Works'. As the East Blue Sea is often plagued by pirates, Baroque Works specialises in, among other things, boarding ships and capturing pirates to collect the promised ransoms. To cut a (rather long) story short, they managed to lure the pirates into a trap by inviting them to a whisky party. According to insiders, Baroque Works has a considerable stock of old casks of Scotch whisky. Hence the capital's name. Anyway, whisky is a big part of Cactus Island and Whiskey Peak.

PEAK WHISKY

WHAT
Japanese whisky

TYPE
Blended whisky

CASK
Sherry

I'm only telling you this to make sure you distinguish 'peak whisky' from the whisky from 'Whiskey Peak'. By the way, in the children's version of this popular computer game, 'Whiskey Peak' has been replaced by 'Misty Peak'.

OK, now that we know all that, I'll take you to 'The Site of Reversible Destiny'.

It's quite a jump. We have to go to Japan, about a hundred kilometres east of Kyoto, to the Yoro area. That is where Madeline Gins and Shusaku Arakawa, two artists and architects, have built an amusement park where visitors can discover that their fate is not unchangeable, but may even be reversible. It's not exactly Disneyland!

You walk through buildings and parks where nothing is exactly horizontal or vertical. The difference between above and below is not always clear, and artificial, false horizons affect your sense of balance and perspective.

I used to feel like this sometimes when I was young and inexperienced and had a bit too much whisky or genever, but on the 'Site', you walk into a new world like a newborn baby, sober and for free.

You must wear sturdy shoes, not stilettos, because the road to Reversible Destiny is often very steep and involves climbing. But that is logic, isn't it?

Why did I bring you to the 'Site'? Not just because it's unforgettable, but mainly because when you enter the park, you have to climb a rocky hill to the top to drink from the 'Yoro spring', said to be the purest water in the world: the water that, according to legend, can turn itself into saké.

The water from which Peak Whisky is made! So what are you waiting for?

Half a century ago, Japanese laws regarding spirits were not very clear. Nor was the Japanese palate easy to define. Saké and shochu distillers tried to produce a liquor that would appeal to the taste buds of 'the man in the street' in the battle against domestic and foreign whiskies. In addition to their classic products, they experimented with herbs and flowers, making sure the new liquor had, to put it mildly, its own 'character'. It all happened on a small scale; if you wanted a bottle, you had to live nearby. Their novelties soon became known as 'ji whiskies'; 'ji' means 'local' or 'regional'.

And business was flourishing. Even more, the government suddenly offered lower taxes on drinks with less than 40 per cent alcohol, and the alcohol content of ji whiskies instantly dropped to 39 per cent and below.

Less alcohol made the liquor cheaper and much easier to drink. As a result, ji whisky experienced a real boom between 1970 and 1980. But, as we've heard so often, great songs don't last long (some, like 'Mamma Mia', last far too long, but that's another story). Instead of keeping things regional, the big producers also tried to grab a part of this market.

Ji whisky quickly lost popularity, and a few decades later, most producers abandoned it. Only two or three small ones remained.

However, during the boom years of ji whisky, the Yoro distillery of Gyokusendo Shuzo tried to sell a full-blown blended whisky based on their own grain and imported malt. Gyokusendo was not on a trial run; the company had started as a saké distillery in 1806 and already had access to the unique Yoro water. Because the company consciously kept production small, its 'Mukade' saké was a sought-after product. The centipede on the label became a symbol of quality. You might not think it of the centipede, but in Japan, it is the epitome of a go-getter who goes all out.

Their 'Peak Whisky' was largely forgotten around the turn of the millennium, but resurfaced in 2018.

Lightly matured in sherry casks.

'Japan's Timeless' adorns the top of the label. It's even stronger than a centipede.

38 Pompeying

Before use, American oak whisky casks are charred on the inside. This can be done in several ways. The cask is often placed horizontally on rollers, without a base or lid. These rollers allow the cask to rotate slowly on its axis while a miniature flamethrower slides inside, charring everything in its path. But the classic method (used mainly in large cooperages) is far more spectacular. The cask, covered at the top, is vertically put over a gas burner built into the floor. After a while, the cover is lifted, creating a vast, piercing flame that chars the whole inside. This is 'pompeying'.

Whoever invented the term must have had the eruption of Mount Vesuvius in 79 AD in mind. It sounds logical: fire, great fire, and searing heat can easily invoke the image of burning Pompeii in romantic souls. But you would have to be a very romantic soul: Pompeii was destroyed in 79 AD by an endless torrent of volcanic ash: rock, dust, cinders and pumice. The city was buried under metres of debris when the first lava flow arrived.

POMPEYING

WHAT

A method of barrel-charring

PURPOSE

To create a unique interaction between alcohol and wood

OK, so that doesn't get us any further.

I found another Pompey who might qualify: Pompeius the Great. He was Julius Caesar's close friend – at least at first. Later, he became his enemy, but that did not stop him from marrying Julius's daughter. A historian tells us: "She was 23 years his junior and was praised for her extraordinary beauty" and "he was on fire for her." Could Pompeius be at the origin of Pompeying? I am tempted to say yes, but I still have my doubts.

I admit, I'll have to owe you the answer.

But don't worry, that will give us plenty of time to move on to the serious questions: Is this charring essential? How long must it burn? Why does it have to burn?

Essential? The casks we get from the USA are made from American oak. In that country, they had (almost) all been used for maturing whisky. In the land of Uncle Sam, the American Bureau of Alcohol, Tobacco, Firearms and Explosives watches over everything. The Bureau states: "Whisky is a distillate of germinated barley or rye, supplemented by not less than 51% corn and/or rye and/or wheat, which [and here it comes] has been aged in charred new barrels."

(But, as in any wonderfully democratic country, this law has at least one loophole: 'light whisky' is also allowed in non-charred casks.) There is no such law in our European whisky countries, but the casks that arrive here have already been charred, and a distiller would have to be crazy not to do it again.

Charring is not an American invention. Long before 1915, when David Lloyd George made it compulsory for Britons to mature whisky in casks for at least three years, some casks used to store flour or herring were already charred. They had discovered that this scorch layer had a beneficial effect against acidification. In whisky, too, the charred layer takes the acidity and bitterness out of the spirit.

How long does it take to char? It is a matter of seconds, although there will always be a cooper who continues for longer. There are usually four stages: stage 1, 15 seconds; stage 2, 30 seconds; stage 3 (the most commonly used), 35 seconds; and stage 4, almost a minute. This last stage is often called 'alligator char', as the charring resembles the skin of this beloved reptile. The longer you char, the deeper the char penetrates, which has different effects on the flavour development of the whisky.

Why char? Oak is almost half cellulose, which is not bad, but cellulose does not react with alcohol, so it has little effect on the spirit. So charring serves some other purpose than the cellulose. Because there's more! 15 per cent of oak is hemicellulose, which is nice. Hemicellulose caramelises when you heat it, giving you sweetness, brown sugar, toffee, and caramel. 25 per cent is lignin. Paper manufacturers hate lignin because they have to remove it from the pulp. But not us: lignin breaks down when heated, giving us vanilla, spice and other welcome flavours. The remaining 10 per cent is made of tannins and lactones, which give the spirit some colour but also bitterness, woody flavours and, fortunately, sometimes coconut.

Connoisseurs claim that 60 to 80 per cent of what you find in your whisky in terms of flavour and aroma is due to the 'wise oak'. Strange, then, that so much praise is given to the water used, the type of barley, the shape of the still, the climate, etc., but so little to the most essential ingredient: the wood.

A friend of mine, a distiller with years of experience in both fields, assures me that distilling genever is much more complex than distilling whisky, because most genevers rarely spend any time in a wooden cask.

Connoisseurs claim that 60 to 80 per cent of what you find in your whisky in terms of flavour and aroma is due to the 'wise oak'.

39 Flee from Rangha

My loyal readers have known it for a long time, and this book has plenty of proof: you will never hear me say a bad word about women. And certainly not about the ladies, young and old, of the whisky industry. I am eternally grateful for what they have done for me, in the distillery and beyond.

I can still see the many dozens of ladies sitting in a huge hall at the Amrut Distillery in Bangalore. All are wearing an identical sari and white gloves. All the newly filled bottles were brought to them and passed from hand to hand around the hall. The first lady would stick a label on it; the next would take the bottle, polish it again and pass it on to a colleague for the next label. And so on, until the bottle ended up in a tube, to be put in a box after another thorough check and more polishing by a few more ladies. Since that day, I have treated every bottle of whisky with awe and gratitude.

FLEE FROM RANGHA

WHO

Rangha leads an army of witches

WHERE

On Bali

AND

She hates alcohol drinkers

But there is one woman I must warn you about. Worse, I would urge you to avoid this woman like the plague. And yes, she does have something to do with alcohol. And no, I swear, I've never met her. All I know is that her name is Rangha.

Because Ketut told me all he knew about Rangha.

I met Ketut a few years ago by chance in Sedimen, a picturesque village in the southeast of Bali. Ketut was a distiller and invited me to his home.

It took a while to find Ketut in Sedimen. There was no need to knock on the door because, like everywhere else on the island, the gate in the fence was wide open. We had to climb a few steps, only to almost run into a metre-high wall. Ketut had built it, and for a good reason: demons and monsters (you can meet them everywhere in Bali) always walk in a straight line. The steps in front of the entrance were the first obstacles for these evil spirits. And if any of them is smart, after dodging the steps, they will definitely run into this wall. Only good ghosts can easily avoid heavy obstacles.

Inside the fence, under the coconut trees, we see three small dwellings and an open space occupied by artfully gilded family temples laden with offerings. The gods are everywhere.

The 'distillery' is beside the temples, under a rusty canopy on four poles. This is where Ketut distils his arrack for the whole family and the many customers in the village.

The word 'arrack' causes confusion in the world of drinks: in Arabic, it means both 'sweat' and 'strong drink'. In the Middle East, arrack is made from dates, plums, figs, etc. In Mongolia, arrack is a delicacy made from fermented horse milk; in Asia Minor, it is a drink made from pure anise. In Indonesia, Batavia Arrack is a distillate of molasses and fermented rice, sometimes with an alcohol content as high as 70 per cent.

For Ketut, however, arrack requires 'tuak' and... his grandfather.

Ketut's grandfather is indispensable in this DIY distillery. Every day, he provides the necessary raw materials, which he collects from the coconut tree flowers. In the morning, he climbs to the top of the tree to cut new flowers. By constantly cutting the flowers, these trees never bear nuts. A sap, which the Balinese call 'tuak', slowly oozes out of the 'wound'. Through a bamboo tube, he channels the sap into a plastic jar tied to the trunk. His day's work is almost done, except that he has to return to the tree in the late afternoon to collect the sap. One flower yields a litre and a half of tuak. Small steps have been cut into the trunks at regular intervals, and Grandpa uses them every time he has to climb the 10-metre-high tree.

"Grandpa is good at this," Ketut says, "especially in the rainy season when the trunk is slippery."

Ketut leaves the sap to ferment in a plastic barrel that can hold about 80 litres. To speed things up, he adds coconut fibre. After about five days, the fermentation is complete, and he can proceed with a 'wash' of about 5 per cent alcohol (which he also calls 'tuak' for convenience).

Now it's time for his 'still'. This one does stand out a lot: the kettle is the hollowed-out base of a palm tree, about a metre high and sealed at the top with a heavy block of wood. The tree's shape makes the base look slightly like a 'wide neck' copper still. The outside is covered with a thick layer of mud, and a metal plate at the bottom prevents the wood fire stoked under the still from setting fire to the whole installation. In the unlikely event that the still breaks down, there is a spare one leaning against the wall. Here, you don't have to wait four years for a new still, the way you'd have to in Scotland.

Two plastic tubes (bought from the electrician) lead the vapours into the 'condenser': the tubes spiral through a barrel of (still) water, ending in a plastic canister. Done.

Distilling once is enough. Apparently.

"From 80 litres of tuak, we get about 10 litres of 40 per cent arrack. If we reduce it to 25 or 30 per cent, we can get up to 20 litres," says Ketut.

Then comes the ultimate moment of truth: tasting.

Ketut: "Arrack was originally distilled only to be offered in small cups to the gods, especially to the evil gods who live underground. That's why we sprinkle it on the floors of our temples. But later on, we learned to drink it ourselves!"

Laughing, he offers me an overflowing glass.

"How much alcohol is that?" I wanted to know.

Ketut looked at me as if this was the most idiotic question he had ever heard.

He waited a moment, clearly doubting whether I was serious, then he calmly took a sip.

"30 per cent," he said, looking into his glass, "maybe 35." Now, that is craftsmanship.

"Do people in Bali drink a lot?" I wanted to know.

He nodded.

"There are several official distilleries that make arrack. The government collects taxes on these, but the vast majority of drinking comes from illegal home distilleries. Not all of them pay the same attention to quality, especially when they produce arrack with a higher alcohol content. Everything that comes out of the still goes into the bottle."

In small villages where arrack is distilled and drunk locally, it often happens that neighbours fall ill suddenly. A few years ago, twenty-five people in one village died within a very short time because they had drunk from the same batch. Blindness caused by methanol poisoning has been reported in many villages. And tourists regularly end up in hospital because – nothing could be more amusing – they have been 'arraking' socially with some locals.

I sip at my glass again, somewhat awkwardly.

"Don't drink too much," he warns, "or you'll have bizarre bad dreams. That is Rangha, the witch demoness, visiting you. Please stay away from her, my friend; stay away from her!"

And then Ketut told me all he knew about Rangha.

What follows is not for sensitive readers, but I will keep it short and sweet.

The demon goddess Rangha is old and widowed. But don't let that fool you: she eats children, leads an army of witches and walks around naked with messy hair and saggy breasts. She has never heard of manicures, and her claws are razor-sharp. Worst of all, she targets men who drink alcohol.

I wonder if she only hates arrack drinkers or (just saying) whisky drinkers, too.

But I have good news for my fellow whisky fans: apart from Rangha, there is also Barong. He's the king of Good Spirits. Like you, he hates Rangha, and they fly at each other's throats regularly. This is good; it keeps her busy, but according to Balinese mythology, this battle always ends in a draw, which doesn't help us any.

So, for your own good, flee from Rangha.

40 Gaelic whisky

Ask a whisky drinker to point out on a map of Scotland exactly where the Glengarioh, Tullibardine or Bladnoch distilleries are located, and they might pause for a moment. On the other hand, ask for Highland Park, Ardbeg or Talisker, and you'll be served with a smile. These island distilleries have an advantage: they are part of the island. Without Scapa or Highland Park, Orkney would never be the same. Take Bowmore off Islay, and you will leave an irreparable scar. Or Talisker from Skye. Like Dunvegan Castle, Talisker is an inseparable part of the island.

Strangely enough, at its inception in 1830, even Talisker was not welcomed there.

GAELIC WHISKY

WHAT

Té Bheag is an example of Gaelic whisky. Té Bheag is a peated blended Scotch whisky with over 40 per cent malt alcohol, bottled in 1976 by Pràban na Linne on the Isle of Skye.

PRONUNCIATION

Chey vek

MEANING

'The little lady' or 'a wee dram'

On the next Lord's Day, the local preacher pounded his fist on his pulpit and shouted that "this establishment at Carbost is one of the greatest curses that could befall this place, the whole island and any other place in the kingdom." Robert Louis Stevenson, author of 'Treasure Island' and 'The Strange Case of Dr Jekyll and Mr Hyde', described Talisker fifty years later as "the king o' drinks".

Today, this water of life still takes the cake for many – so much so that we often think it is the only distillery on Skye. And that's not true.

And what's more, Skye isn't even called Skye anymore. Yes, I know, after four or five whiskies, we were still singing at the top of our lungs: "Speed, bonnie boat, like a bird on the wing, ...over the sea to Skye."

Ridiculous: since April 2007, the island has officially been called Eilean a' Cheo, which means 'Island in the Mist'. That was the government's decision. Given that a third of the 9,000 inhabitants speak Gaelic, the country's leaders thought a Gaelic name would look better than an 'Anglicised slave name'.

On the other hand, the people of Skye were not too happy about this, as the proper, ancient Gaelic name of the island is An 't-Eilean Sgitheanach, which means 'winged island'.

That aside. Do you agree that I should stick with 'Skye' anyway?

We owe the fact that the extinct Gaelic on Skye was brought back to life to one man ...and his whisky: Sir Iain Noble and his 'Té Bheag Unchillfiltered Blended Whisky'.

Iain Andrew Noble was the son of a British diplomat married to the daughter of a Norwegian ambassador. He was born in Berlin in 1935. With such parents, he only stayed at the same school briefly. He was educated in China and Argentina and then sent off to England. He went to Eton and Oxford and studied Gaelic in Edinburgh. He was clever, a hard worker, a good businessman and – very helpfully – rich. He founded the very first commercial bank in Scotland, just for starters. In 1972, Iain bought an estate of no less than eight thousand acres on Skye with a hotel and an early nineteenth-century farmstead known as Sabhal Mòr Ostaig.

There, he established the first Gaelic school: Gaelic College. This was the start of his crusade to revive the island's original Celtic language. He fought friend and foe alike, and managed to ensure that all the signs on the island were in Gaelic. In 1976, he became an independent bottler named Pràban na Linne, marketing an authentic 'Gaelic whisky'. His first products were 'Té Bheag', 'MacNaMara' and 'Poit Dhubh'. The first two are blended whiskies, while the last is a blended malt. All were nicely smoked and (a rarity) were not chill-filtered. All the labels were in Gaelic, which the Scotch Whisky Association could live with, but the phrase 'Gaelic Whisky' on the bottle (instead of 'Scotch Whisky') was a step too far.

This did not stop Sir Iain Noble from dreaming of his own Gaelic distillery, where not only the whisky but also the language on the shop floor would be Gaelic. He died in 2010, however, before the necessary renovation and building work could begin on his Sabhal Mòr Ostaig estate.

Mossburn Distillers, which began bottling in 2013, took up Noble's plan and, in 2017, brought a new Skye whisky to the Isle of Skye: Torabheag. Talisker is no longer the only one. Moreover, Mossburn is now part of the Swedish group Haydn Holding, so Gaelic has not become the working language within the company.

Nevertheless, Sir Iain Noble played a masterful role in the history of Scotch whisky and the preservation and revival of the islands' language. He was rightly awarded the title of Officer of the Most Excellent Order of the British Empire.

It is also thanks to him that we now often bite our tongues at those damned difficult names of Scottish distilleries and malts. Bruichladdich, Craighellachie, Pittyvaich, Bunnahabhain... what will they think of next?

If I can help, here you go: 'bh' and 'mh' are 'v', 'ph' is 'f', 'fh' and 'ch' are 'h', 'chd' sounds like 'chk', 'gh' and 'dh' are 'y'. Remember that you don't always have to pronounce these letters, and sometimes you need to add vowels where there are none. Have you got it?

But I don't want to bother you any further with this; I've probably already broken your illusion at the beginning of this piece by revealing that Skye is not actually called Skye.

Well, I still held back. I kept saying, for example, that Talisker is an 'island whisky'. As if it were perfectly normal. Well, while we're at it, Skye is technically not an island.

The generally accepted definition of an island is given by Hamish Haswell-Smith in his masterpiece 'The Scottish Islands': "An island is a piece of land, or group of pieces of land, which at the lowest astronomical tide is entirely surrounded by seawater and to which there is no permanent dry access."

Skye has been connected to the 'mainland' by a bridge since 16 October 1995. And you'll agree, a bridge counts as 'permanent dry access'.

That hurts! I know.

But don't worry, folks.

If (like me now) you fancy a Talisker, then pour yourself one of those delicious island whiskies. Slainte!

In 1976, he became an independent bottler named Pr.ban na Linne, marketing an authentic 'Gaelic whisky'.

41 The Coles Distillery

Above the entrance to the distillery, which is a building that looks more like a newly built barn with a neat driftwood gate, hangs a large sign depicting some daffodils and this unmistakable text:

"IN MEMORY OF TRACIA ANNE COLES WHO IS NOW ONLY RESPONSIBLE FOR THE 'ANGELS' SHARE' - 1944-2012"

Sadly, I was never lucky enough to meet Tracia, who died of cancer, but after an hour's conversation with her two sons, I tried to picture her on my way out. She must have been a tall, buxom, sturdy woman with sparkling eyes, a sense of humour, smile lines around her mouth and a look that betrayed innovative ideas. I could be wrong, of course, but I was convinced I was right, having seen that she had passed on all these gifts to her two sons and even her granddaughters.

THE COLES DISTILLERY

WHAT
The most unconventional whisky distillery

WHERE
Llanddarog in South Wales

MOTTO
If it gets you drunk, we'll make it!

The Coles's story actually begins with a thatched roof. In 1994, the family was planning to build a new house, and there was one condition: it had to have a thatched roof. That wasn't uncommon in Wales, so the Coles decided to look around. In Llanddarog, about thirty kilometres north-west of Swansea, the White Hart Inn is a perfect example: a beautiful roof on a pub that dates back to 1371. As they admire the roof, one of them pointed to the sign on the door: 'FOR SALE'. So they bought The White Hart Inn and forgot about the building plans. It marked the start of a small business, 'family run' in the broadest sense.

Marcus and his wife Jessica ran the pub, while Marcus's brother Cain ran the bar, and daughters Annabelle and Angelica were recruited as waitresses. But that was not the end of it. Marcus and Cain soon extended their activities to brewer, cider maker, winemaker, master distiller, master blender, marketeer, graphic designer, bottler, labeller, etc. In other words, they did it all themselves.

The pub, once one of the many haunts of the famous Welsh poet Dylan Thomas, resumed its previous success and welcomed many celebrities. In 2003, when he was still Crown Prince, Charles dropped in and poured himself a pint of Cwcw Blasus, pronounced 'coucou blasus', a tasty beer brewed in-house, as the pub had added a brewery in 1999.

That wasn't all they served, either: since 2011, hundreds of kilos of apples have been harvested yearly in October to make fine champagne cider.

And that was just the start of a long story.

We meet Marcus and Cain in their headquarters, a corner of the pub next to a wee shop where all their products are displayed. Marcus folds up his laptop and pushes aside a roll of labels. This 'office' is also where their jars and bottles are labelled.

“How did you get into whisky?” we asked.

Marcus: “When we wanted to do something new and didn’t know how, we looked it up on the internet. One day, we wanted to make whisky! And rum. And vodka. And gin. And brandy. We didn’t even have a still. (He laughs.) We contacted companies that made stills and found two willing to help us: one in Germany and one in Chicago. As neither of us spoke German, it became a trip to the USA. We set off with the idea of getting a 200-300 litre still, but soon learned that if you are a small distillery, you need a big still. Ours is now about 3,000 litres. We also learnt that making a still that can distil all kinds of distillates is not easy. So we went home with the firm belief that making our own still ourselves was better.”

Cain, an engineer by training, sat at the drawing board and roughly sketched out his own still: a pot still connected to two column stills. All made of... stainless steel!

“Copper needs far too much cleaning work!” says Marcus.

Only the twenty invisible plates in each column and the rectifiers are made of copper. To verify if the design would work, a local craftsman was hired to build the whole structure on a scale of one to five. And it worked perfectly! They easily

The Coles brothers with their own take on distilling ↓

produced alcohol of 96 per cent. Another advantage was that the pot still could be used separately, as could the two column stills, or any combination of the three.

The next step was obvious: build it all full-sized.

They talked to Forsyth and other well-known still builders, but nobody would accept the order. The concept of this 'Coles still' was too far out of their comfort zone. Fortunately, a small company in Oxford took the plunge. It came with a price tag of about 1.2 million pounds.

Meanwhile, the brothers solved another problem: constructing a building eight metres tall in their tiny village. Even next to their historic pub would have been a waste, so they dug a huge pit, four metres deep, and built the distillery mostly underground.

When it was all over, the Coles, relieved, took a holiday to Jamaica. That was clearly premeditated. They visited the famous Hampden rum distillery and peppered everyone they met with questions. The Jamaicans were astonished at their curiosity, but Marcus reassured them: "We just want to make our own rum at home."

So rum, made from molasses and yeast from Jamaica, was the first spirit to flow from the still.

"And made with water from Wales!" laughs Marcus.

And then, COVID-19 came along.

Wales has few distilleries. When the coronavirus struck, the government begged for assistance from anyone who could produce alcohol. Coles switched to pure alcohol and managed to make 1,000 litres a day.

"This is our `organic' whisky," Marcus explains. "We didn't actually plan to make it; organic is way too expensive.

Marcus explains, "We could handle two or three runs a day, partly because of the size of our still but mainly because of the basic rule we set ourselves: if we install something, it has to work fast. For example, the pipes in the distillery that carry the steam are three times thicker than in a traditional distillery. This allows us to heat the wash three times faster! We bought them very cheaply on eBay, brand new!"

"Now, thankfully, things can settle down a bit," he continues. "We work here every day from four in the morning until noon because that's when the pub opens, and we're needed there."

We taste one of their whisky creations, a malt whisky from a distillery where not a square inch of copper can be seen. In the past, we have read many claims about such things that are less than encouraging. But this 'Coles' is surprising: creamy and fruity, with some vanilla and a pronounced wood note. It's pretty tasty.

"This is our 'organic' whisky," Marcus explains. "We didn't actually plan to make it; organic is way too expensive. But they brought us the wrong batch of barley, and we didn't pay attention. This whisky was matured first in a bourbon cask and then in a red wine cask."

Does he make red wine, too?

Marcus nods: "If it gets you drunk, we'll make it!"

The Coles Distillery ↓

42 Kiwi-whisky

Back in the days when I was copywriting for a living, I remember a campaign for a fashion chain to highlight the latest styles of men's and women's clothing for the upcoming summer season. Because of the 'new colours', they insisted on a photo shoot featuring the summer highlands of Scotland. No problem, of course, except that the shoot occurred in the depths of winter. It was bitterly cold in the snowy Highlands at the time.

KIWI-WHISKY

WHAT

Whiskies from New Zealand

SPECIAL FEATURES

Lax legislation on alcohol distillation, and probably the only country that lowered the legal drinking age from 21 to 18

But in the world of advertising, everything is possible. The photographer and models flew to South Island in New Zealand, which was then in high summer. The climate is the same as in Scotland, and the landscape looks like the Scottish Highlands. Dunedin, the South Island's second-largest city, is said to be the most Scottish city outside of Scotland and even bears the former name of Edinburgh. Many street names are reminiscent of Scotch whisky, and the chances of meeting a Mac... or Mc... are exceptionally high.

In other words, if you're a whisky lover and don't like it here anymore, grab your duffel bag and head for New Zealand.

Still waiting? Well, New Zealand has a lot of water, a lot of barley and a lot of peat.

Understood? No? Look, this will convince you: anyone can make whisky in New Zealand! At home! No licence, no excise duty.

New Zealand's Customs and Excise Act 1996 speaks at length about excise duty and licensing of tobacco, beer, wine, and spirits. But section 68B of that long text opens a back door with the 'exemption for personal use'. This text clearly states that the law does not apply to the production of spirits in a person's private home or residence as long as the spirits are produced for personal use.

That's a lot different from the rules in Australia. There, the law is clear: anyone who possesses, buys, sells, manufactures or disposes a still of more than 5 litres is committing an offence and liable to a hefty fine.

If the Kiwis (as New Zealanders like to call themselves) are looking for a complete installation in their own home, it's hardly any effort: they can buy everything and find plenty of instructions online.

There are countless home distilleries. Not all of them make whisky; some stick to gin or vodka, while others work with herbs and fruits.

Could this be why we find so few commercial Kiwi whiskies in our whisky books? Are there any commercial distilleries left in New Zealand?

The last whisky distillery in New Zealand closed its doors in 1997: Willowbank. It was not only known as 'the southernmost distillery in the world' but also as the producer of the world's worst whisky. No wonder: its stills were made of stainless steel. Seagram took over in 1981 and replaced the stills with copper ones. Their Lammerlaw whisky enjoyed better press coverage.

GUARANTEED
Ergo Bibamus
Free from
POISONS
OLD HOKONUI
Passed All Tests except the Police
Bottled by ME for YOU
Produce of SOUTHLAND.
Supplied to all Snake Charmers
ORIGINAL
Southland Grain Spirit 40% alc/vol 375mls

However, when a massive order from South Korea in 1995 backfired, Seagram sold the whole business. The new owner dismantled everything and sold the stills to a rum distiller. Some intelligent guys managed to snap up the 443 full casks, still in the warehouses. They later formed the New Zealand Whiskey Company and still release the old Lammerlaw from time to time, albeit renamed Milford.

But New Zealand's whisky story did not end there. Over the past twenty years, craft distilleries popped up like mushrooms, and there are now more than 150.

This marks the start of a new chapter in a story that, strangely enough, began in the late nineteenth century in... Scotland! Landowners robbed thousands of small farmers of their homes and land to make way for sheep, which would fetch much more: the infamous 'Highland Clearances'. The Great Famine from 1845 to 1850 made matters even worse, forcing even the hardiest Scottish homesteaders to flee. They emigrated in large numbers to America, Canada, Australia and New Zealand.

One of these 'clearance refugees' was Mary McRae, a widow with seven children. She arrived in Dunedin in 1872 with three brothers and a small copper still. She distilled her unnamed, illicit whisky in the Hokonui hills, which eventually became so well known that everyone knew that 'Hokonui' was synonymous with 'moonshine'.

The only annoying thing about the whole affair was that, at the time, no one was allowed to distil alcohol without a licence. In the years of prohibition that followed, the government's hunt for liquor offenders was a significant occupation. Hokonui Moonshine fell silent, and stocks were exhausted. Rare bottles became prized collectors' items.

But Hokonui lived on in Kiwis' memories. In 2001, the Hokonui Moonshine Museum opened in Gore, and four years later, the Southern Distilling Company was formed to market Old Hokonui Moonshine, made entirely from Mother McRae's recovered recipe.

Now, the bottle has a label with the name, a skull, and crossed knives. This refers to the time when everything was off-limits.

The bottom line is: "Passed all tests, except the police."

43 Bootleggers' hooch

Early one morning in 1927, police raided the home of octogenarian Lavinia Gilman in northern Montana, near the Canadian border. They had long suspected her and, to their delight, found over a 1,000 litres of illegally distilled whisky. As usual, a neighbour of Lavinia's had come over to help her with the distillation.

We are right in the middle of Prohibition in America. Back then, you could make a certain amount of wine and cider for your own use, but brewing beer or distilling whisky was out of the question.

BOOTLEGGERS' HOOCH

WHAT
During Prohibition, bootleggers smuggled the banned drink to their customers

NAME
The word 'bootlegger' indicates the tricks they used, often hiding the whisky in their boots or tied around their legs

HOOCH
Illegally distilled whisky

Her still and whisky were confiscated, and Lavinia had to appear in court. The judge advised her to get her son to admit that he had distilled the whisky. The judge was convinced that women could not handle that.

He was not the only one persuaded that whisky-making was a man's job. Hadn't the head of the New York Women's Police Department said the year before that women were incapable of distilling alcohol illegally?

Therefore, even when women stubbornly insisted that they were making it themselves but had a good reason for doing so ('their children were starving', etc.), they were usually not punished, or got off much more lightly than men. Women had another advantage in this 'Wild West': in most

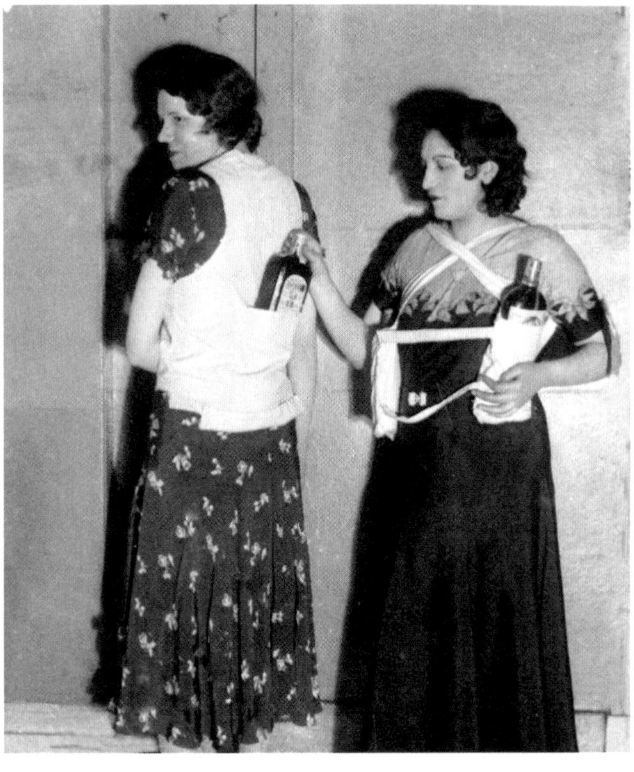

states, it was illegal to search women. As a result, we not only find women who prepared the stuff at home, but also a large group of female couriers who used the most cunning tricks to get the forbidden devil's drink to the craving drinkers.

We are entering the era of the moonshiner and the bootlegger.

The legendary Prohibition of the early 20th century was no surprise to Americans. By 1880, Kansas had declared itself an 'alcohol-free state', and by 1920, when Prohibition became the norm, 33 of the then 48 states were 'dry'. Many institutions and groups, including the Nonconformist Churches and many Women's Temperance Movements, had fought for this.

One of the results of this struggle was that the number of saloons and bars in New York was reduced by seven thousand. By 1918, there were 'barely' 12,000. These were all venerable institutions where gentlemen met, smoked and drank. At best, there was a small, austere room at the back where the ladies and children could sit away from the harmful liquor.

Some 15 years later, at the end of Prohibition, there were 32,000 illegal saloons in New York. Often hidden behind nondescript facades, with a simple door where the visitor could softly (easily) mumble the password and enter, these were the speakeasies. Men and women were allowed in, the moonshine whisky was poured smoothly, sometimes by scantily clad beauties, and in case of need, you could opt for other sinful acts.

Gangsters like 'The Big Fellow' Al Capone and Lucky Luciano were often behind these cosy gold mines, but women also owned several businesses. Texas Guinan, 'The Queen of the Nightclubs', and Belle Livingstone would achieve eternal fame by skilfully running their 'blind tigers' or 'blind pigs', as these illegal watering holes were known.

But where did they get the hooch? Hooch is another of the many colourful terms that surfaced during Prohibition: it means much the same as moonshine: illegally distilled alcohol.

Of course, much of that era's American whisky was distilled clandestinely in remote or well-hidden places in the USA. In 1921, the first year of Prohibition, more than 95,000 distilleries were discovered. By 1930, that rose to more than 282,000! The 'drink of the gods' they produced was not always of the highest quality, often containing suspicious amounts of fuel oil, methanol, ammonium oxalate and various other substances that might be found in a car battery.

These were the 'small fish' in this massive pond of illegal alcohol. Not only did they have to produce the hooch, but they also had to sell the fruits of their labour. They were the real bootleggers, using the most straightforward and surprising tricks to get past the inspections. Most of them were women, both at the stills and on the road.

Take Maggie Bailey from Clovertown, Kentucky, the 'Queen of the Mountain Bootleggers'. She started distilling when she was seventeen and made it her life's work. She never sold to teenagers or drunks and saw no reason to stop when Prohibition ended. She distilled and sold moonshine until she was ninety. Or Black Bertie Brown, who kept her family rolling in money and only stopped when her kettle exploded in 1933.

Vast quantities of Scotch, Canadian and other whiskies also poured into the country.

The border between the United States and Canada is 6,400 kilometres long, and if you add the border with Mexico and all the coastlines, the total is more than 30,000 kilometres. Imagine keeping track of that, day in and day out, with only three thousand agents at your disposal. Working eight-hour shifts, each of them would have to cover 30 kilometres at a time. In Cuba, the Bahamas, Bermuda, Canada, Belize (then British Honduras), etc., boys stood ready to bring the precious liquid to the US coast.

Boys? There were some handy ladies, too!

→ Gertrude Lythgoe

Gertrude Lythgoe was one of them. This beauty was nicknamed 'Cleo' because she resembled Cleopatra, an admirable trait she used to her advantage. Cleo was American, but moved to the city of Nassau in the Bahamas at the start of Prohibition, where she imported the best Scotch whiskies. Her motto was, 'I don't need a man to tell me what to do', and she refused all marriage proposals. She built her own fleet and hired sailors to take her whiskies to America. All this made her a fortune. According to some sources, she was a dollar millionaire by 1925. In the same year, however, she was caught, and her business was put to an end.

Her 'colleague', Spanish Marie, whose real name was Marie Waite, also owned 15 boats that brought the precious goods from Cuba to Miami and Key West. Marie specialised in rum but was also active in other areas. She married gangster Charlie Waite, who was in the same business. He was killed in 1926, and Marie continued his operations. Increasingly troubled by the Coast Guard's speedboats, she started her own radio station, using their wavelength, constantly broadcasting false information and sending the Coast Guard in all directions. When she was caught, she simply paid the fine and carried on. When Prohibition ended and her trade became obsolete, Marie took on a new challenge: she became the first female automobile mechanic in Florida.

Proving the head of the New York Woman's Police Department wrong, "Women can do men's work," she said.

Finally, let us all admit in unison that we whisky people owe much to women.

Since the Middle Ages, women have been looking after beer and other hooch. Sadly, nearly three thousand witches were burned in Scotland in the sixteenth and seventeenth centuries. They were said to dance with the devil and to know how to make potions from herbs and other ingredients to intoxicate people.

How much knowledge was lost with those women?

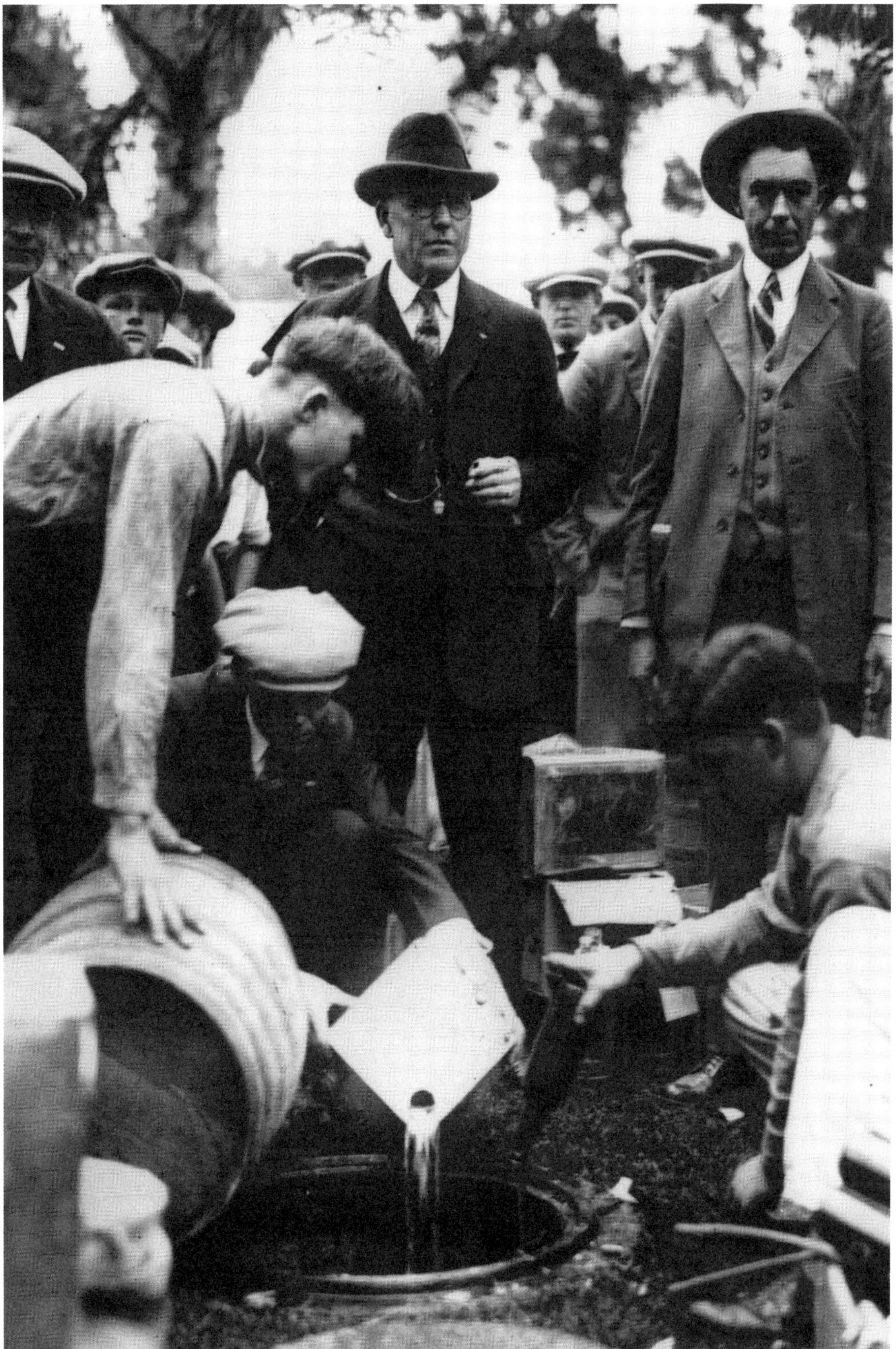

44 ABV

"They dragged Hypatia of Alexandria to the Caesareum, stripped her, killed her and cut up her body with the shards of a broken jug."

Although I have never done it myself (honest!), I can vividly imagine the first part of the above. But don't ask me how they did it with the shards because I have no idea. It's not explained in the book I just quoted from, either. It's a thick book, though.

Anyway, Hypatia is dead, and that's a pity.

Because Hypatia, who lived in the fourth century, was a clever woman. As far as we know, she was the very first woman in the history of mathematics. Among other things, she was also a philosopher, a physicist, and an astronomer and (if we rely on the drawings in the books) certainly good at other things, too. But that's departing from the topic at hand. Let's concentrate on what she could mean for our whisky.

Well, Hypatia knew the 'Law of Archimedes'. Archimedes is that bloke from the fourth century BC who filled his bathtub to the brim, crawled into it, and was amazed that the thing overflowed. Eureka!

His law was: 'A body immersed in a liquid experiences an upward pressure equal to the weight of the displaced liquid'.

Based on this, Hypatia had a floater made that could measure how deep it sank in a mixture of water and sugar. This allowed her to work out the density of the mixture and, from that, how much sugar was in it. Clever, eh?

We now call such a floater a 'hydrometer' and whisky books usually state that the Brit Bartholomew Sikes invented it.

And you know I never argue with the British.

In 1818, the British Parliament declared in the Hydrometer Act that the Sikes hydrometer (obviously a 'modern' version of the Hypatia floater) would be the only official instrument for determining alcohol content.

ABV

WHAT

Alcohol by volume

DEFINITION

The number of millilitres of ethyl alcohol in 100 millilitres of an alcoholic beverage, measured at 20°C

IMPORTANT

With ABV, you know where you stand as a drinker, and the tax authorities know how much tax they can add

Finally, we had a way to determine the ratio of 'alcohol by volume' or ABV. This was a godsend for excise officers, giving them a reliable tool to collect sufficient excise.

One hundred sixty years later, the International Organisation of Legal Metrology proposed the universal use of the ABV system. Europe agreed, but the rest of the world was reluctant to abandon the old system of 'proof'.

The idea of 'proof' dates back to the late Middle Ages. People would mix an explosive with some alcohol to see if it fizzled, burned, or exploded, determining the different degrees of proof.

However, the modern definition of 'proof' can be found in the UK Customs and Excise Act of 1952.

Take a deep breath and then decide that you want to forget this as soon as possible: “A spirit drink shall be deemed to be ‘proof’ if the volume of ethyl alcohol contained in it, when added to the volume of the spirit drink with distilled water, is equal in weight to up to twelve-thirteens of a volume of distilled water equal to the volume of the spirit drink, the volume of each liquid being calculated at a temperature of 51°F or 10.5°C.”

In other words, you have a bottle of whisky and the same bottle of water, and you crawl into your cellar (because of the temperature). You weigh the two contents. If the weight of your whisky is 0.923 times the weight of the water, your whisky is 100% proof.

Fortunately, someone immediately thought of a comparison table based on the idea that 100% ABV equals 175° proof. So, you multiply the percentage ABV by 1.75, and you always get the proof. Or, if you want to work the other way around, starting from proof, you multiply the number of degrees proof by 0.571, and you get the ABV.

At least if you mean ‘UK proof’.

But if you mean USA proof, it is not 1.75 times, but two times. They equate pure alcohol with 200° proof. To make things even more fun, the French have introduced a third system, an idea of the scientist Joseph-Louis Gay-Lussac: he asserts that 100° proof equals 100% ABV. So, 40% ABV is 40° proof.

After reading all this, you might be tempted to kiss Hypatia on the forehead in gratitude for her efforts with the hydrometer.

After all, it's true. Just keep it simple, use only ABV! Like in Europe.

Well, be happy because there are calls worldwide for a general switch to ABV.

But not everyone is happy about it. On the other side of the ocean, some level-headed Americans want to introduce 'SD': the 'Standard Drink'. The bottle would tell you exactly how much alcohol is in one SD. If you drank five SDs, for example, you would know (to the decimal point) exactly how much alcohol you had ingested.

Of course, you now ask, "How big is one SD?" Good question. It varies from drink to drink, of course. For whisky, it is 1.5 ounces; for beer, 12 ounces; for wine, 5 ounces...

How much is an ounce? Well, there are four ounces in circulation: the 'British Imperial fluid ounce', the 'United States customary fluid ounce', the 'United States food labelling fluid ounce' and the 'International Avoirdupois ounce'. None differs by more than a millilitre, and they all hover around 29 ml.

But beware: we are not there yet! The specific alcohol content of your bottle must also be considered.

Wait a moment...What do you think? Shouldn't we stick to ABV?

What a mess! In the long run, it'll drive you to drink.

'To measure is to know', as the old saying goes.

Give me a break.

However, the modern definition of `proof' can be found in the UK Customs and Excise Act of 1952.

45 The whisky capsule storm

On a Monday morning in 2019, Nina Caplan, editor of 'The Guardian', was pretty fired up. In her anger, she even referred to Dr Frankenstein and Willy Wonka, the genius boss of 'The Chocolate Factory'.

Anyone who has enjoyed a proper education knows that Willy Wonka created chewing gum with the flavours of a three-course meal: soup, meatloaf, and blueberries. The flavours were released slowly, one after the other. Violet Beauregarde, a young visitor addicted to chewing gum, stuffed her mouth with it and turned blue and swollen like a blueberry.

THE WHISKY CAPSULE STORM

WHAT
The Glenlivet is introducing 'whisky capsules'

RELEASE DATE
October 2019

CONSEQUENCE
A minor Twitter riot

This led the editor seamlessly to the source of her wrath: Speyside's Glenlivet distillery had just launched whisky cocktails in capsules. "Perhaps they could fill their next set of capsules with a salty snack and an aspirin!" she said.

That would be a relief; it speaks for itself.

But she wasn't the only one: ABC News didn't put it quite so bluntly, but suggested that a sick mind must have been behind it. They called on then-Prime Minister Nicola Sturgeon to intervene in this worthless 'shit'. And Twitter users tripped over each other to bash the whole thing and list all the drawbacks of this despicable marketing move.

In reality, it was nothing more than a tempest in a teacup. I admit that it is an unfortunate expression because one of the problems was that no cup was involved. You only had to put the capsule in your mouth and break it.

The shell was made of seaweed and was perfectly digestible. Glenlivet hired a young company called Nopla to do the job. Nopla was developing alternatives to plastic, and their capsules already offered a solution. For example, they had already produced water capsules for marathon runners. A marathon runner needs water but does not want to nibble on a capsule on the way. Don't worry, just spit the capsule out on the side of the road no trace will be left just a few days later. No one will be able to mourn it anyway.

The contents of the whisky capsules... that's something else.

Glenlivet asked the specialists at Tayēr+Elementary cocktail bar on London's Old Street to produce three cocktails based on their whisky, with 'citrus, wood and spice' as their respective characters. Tayēr+Elementary is no slouch! They are known for their inventive new flavour bombs, so we can't accuse them of shoddy quality. So, the capsules were OK to be drunk – ahem, eaten.

However, the buzz around the whisky capsules didn't linger long, and no wonder. They were only available as an appetiser or 'amuse-gueule' for ten days, and in only one bar: the Tayēr+Elementary, of course, during 'London Cocktail Week' 2019. You could not buy them or put them in your pocket. Swallow on the spot was the message.

But despite the 'local' success, it remained, as initially intended, just this one experiment. The Glenlivet just wanted to show that it was OK to think outside the box in the old-fashioned world of whisky.

So, friends, rest assured: there will be no whisky capsule trends. But it just shows that we have yet to see the end of it.

I have long harboured the thought that someone would one day come up with a non-alcoholic whisky. That is something we never had.

I was kidding, of course. But all these jokes, like those from the masterful mind of Roald Dahl, are too imaginative to be true one day.

For example, Willy Wonka's 'three-course chewing gum' was also a nice invention. But...

Wait a minute.

Have you ever heard of the Institute of Food Research in Norwich, England? These guys are concerned about your and my health, so they test everything on the market and help to find new healthy, nutritious and safe treats.

They are studying a lot of colloidosomes right now. As I understood, these are filled microcapsules. The shell of these capsules is constructed to stay intact until the temperature and acidity around it reach the correct ratio. Only then will the thing burst and release its contents. By manipulating the shell, you can make one microcapsule burst earlier than the others.

So if you put three of these microcapsules in a stick of chewing gum and make one burst a little earlier than the others, you get... yes... a three-course-chewing gum. Imagine: first, you get a prawn croquette, then an Irish rib-eye steak and finally a chocolate moelleux.

Note: we are almost there. They only have to figure out how to get rid of the crappy taste of the croquette before the rib-eye arrives.

But even that will not be long!

Flying on a budget airline will never have been so delicious: first a whisky in powder form with a glass of water, then a three-course chewing gum.

With a vegetarian option, of course.

46 Woman + whisky

Although it was long ago, I still remember a day out with friends. Cosy with a glass on a terrace and a nice chat, we were four couples: four men and four women. That's the way it was in the old days. The conversation turned to a mutual friend who had started a business and managed to build it up to an excellent level quickly.

One of the ladies remarked that he was lucky that his wife had played a significant part in it.

WOMAN + WHISKY

WHAT

In recent decades, more and more women have become involved in whisky, both as consumers and producers

AND

They needed to get more attention in the whisky press

↑ Aista Philips, Penderin I

Then, with a sweet look in my direction, my wife said, "What would men be without women?"

I was young and inexperienced in marital dialogue, so I replied jokingly and hesitantly, "Maybe... happier?"

I shouldn't have done that!

Now I know that it was a rhetorical question to which no answer was expected, let alone an idiotic one like mine. But I must admit, now that I am much older, I realise it was not so absurd after all.

And many years later, as I sat meditating over a glass of Old Pulteney, the question suddenly arose: "Where would our whisky world be today without women?"

Forty years ago, when I started studying whisky, it was an impregnable man's world. The first women to break the barrier were the 'drivers', bringing their husbands to master classes and whisky festivals, without understanding what made them so happy to be there, and taking them safely home afterwards.

But that soon changed. In the distilleries, too, there are more women now, and not just behind the counter. It's easy to find a female blender, a female marketing manager, a female brand ambassador, or a female master distiller. Nice, isn't it?

I admit, women are much better than men at tasting, describing flavours, etc. Then again, men are so much better at so many other things...

Stop it, idiot, or didn't you learn anything, with your silly jokes?

But whisky women rarely get more than a few lines in whisky books and stories. We know Helen Comming, widow of Cardow founder John Comming, who ran the distillery herself in 1864. And Bessie Williamson of Laphroaig is no stranger to us either, but that's it.

That's why we are here: proud to present two ladies who rarely make it to the stage.

Dr Sonat Birnecker Hart is the owner and CEO of

Koval Distillery in Chicago. Sonat spent more than a decade as a professor of history at universities in Germany and the United States. She left academia in 2008 to found Koval. The first distillery in Chicago since Prohibition, it is the only distillery in America (and possibly the world?) where women run everything. Koval markets six different organic whiskies, quickly reaching over fifty countries and winning over a hundred awards. Sonat also founded Kothe Distilling Technologies, a spirits industry consultancy that helps budding 'craft' distillers get off the ground, and has trained more than three thousand newcomers to the whisky industry.

She has been inducted into the Disciples d'Escoffier and named Illinois Small Business Person of the Year for her efforts in the distilling industry.

With such a record, she is justifiably proud.

And then there is Catherine Spears Frye Carpenter, who rewrote the entire history of American whiskey with a smallish piece of paper. Written in 1818, it explains in simple terms how to use 'sour mash' to make whiskey. Some have claimed she did not write that paper, but we're not fooled. We must admit, however, that she took her inspiration from the rum world. There, 'sour mash' was used as far back as the seventeenth century. The oldest written reference to rum, a work from 1650, describes the production process.

Rum people don't use the expression 'sour mash' but 'dunder'. The word is derived from the Spanish 'redundar', which means 'leftover' or 'surplus'. And that is exactly what 'sour mash' is. It's like using sourdough to make bread.

The principle is simple: you save a bit of the last fermented mash and add it to the new wort to be fermented. Not only does this ensure consistency in the final result, but it also provides better acidity control, prevents bacterial contamination and combats wild yeasts.

Rum people don't use the expression 'sour mash' but 'dunder'. The word is derived from the Spanish 'redundar', which means 'leftover' or 'surplus'.

Only a few US distilleries proudly display the term 'sour mash' on their labels, but in fact, almost all distilleries in the USA use it.

Contrary to what the term 'sour mash' might suggest, this method does not make the whisky more acidic. On the contrary, it produces more esters and aldehydes, adding flavours such as caramel, vanilla, fruit and spices.

Fly to the famous Hampden Distillery in Jamaica to learn how this system is used in rum distilleries. In the rum industry, the sour mash is allowed to evolve in the open air. They even add organic material, such as overripe fruit, while encouraging decomposition.

You won't need to ask where to find their dunder stock; all you have to do is follow your nose and the trail of the pungent smell. But don't worry; the distillation process ensures that these unpleasant odours give way to a mass of fruity esters, which is why Jamaican rum is so famous.

47 De Frongoch Distillery

DE FRONGOCH DISTILLERY

WHERE
On the edge of Snowdonia, near Bala, in Wales

SIGNIFICANCE
The first and only distillery in Wales, until the 21st century

POINTS OF INTEREST
Frongoch Distillery was the birthplace of the the Irish Republican Army or IRA

Anyone travelling from Shrewsbury to Snowdonia in Wales should take the A4212 at Bala. Not just because it is a quiet and photogenic road, but because it takes you past a place that has played an essential part in the history of whisky in Wales and an even more critical part in the history of the United Kingdom: Frongoch. Don't expect too much: it's just some scattered houses, two of which stand out because they are taller and more spacious than the others. But the place I am talking about is itself little more than a patch of meadow. This was once the site of the Frongoch Distillery, and the two remarkable houses were its headquarters and manager's house, more than a century ago.

It was not until 1889 that the first distillery in Wales was established. Two wealthy friends (including Lloyd Prince, owner of the now Grade II listed Riwlas Estate in Bala) put their heads together. They pooled their resources to build the

The Welsh Whisky Distillery Company Limited (in Liquidation)

To the Registrar of Joint Stock Companies
House
London

Sir,
We beg to inform you that a Final Meeting of the above named Company was duly held on Thirtieth day of September 1903 for the purpose of having an account laid before them, shewing the manner in which the winding up of the Company has been Conducted and the property of the Company disposed of, and the same was done accordingly.

Dated the 30th day of September 1903.

Liquidators

distillery: 100,000 pounds (about 10 million today). It was a state-of-the-art distillery from the outset, with maturing warehouses, peat storage, accommodation for thirty staff and their families and, of course, modest premises for the excise officer. The location was also perfect, with plenty of water nearby, plenty of peat, fertile fields and a well-maintained railway line.

Even before the requirement of 'at least three years' maturing' was introduced, they let the whisky mature for at least five years before bottling.

Now, the Scots would be astonished!

Queen Victoria must have heard about Frongoch, because she stood on their doorstep two years later. Both the Queen and the Prince of Wales had a nose for whisky. They were welcomed with open arms and offered a full cask each, which they accepted – as monarchs do – without protest. At the Frongoch distillery, they took this gentle gesture from the Queen and Prince as proof that they were now 'purveyors to the court'. And so, in 1895, they launched their 'masterpiece': a five-year-old peated malt whisky: Royal Welsh Whisky. They put the 'Royal' on it, but as far as I know, no document has ever been found in which the British monarchs granted their 'Royal Warrant'. No one seemed overly concerned about that, however; Royal Welsh Whisky caught on, sold like hotcakes, and demand grew.

But many years before the Frongoch Distillery was established, a worldwide temperance movement had started, a battle against alcohol. And Wales would not escape its backlash. The finger of blame was always pointed at the working-class drinkers, who supposedly needed to be protected. As early as 1881, pubs in Wales had to close on Sundays, and the movement grew. In 1901, the Women's Temper-

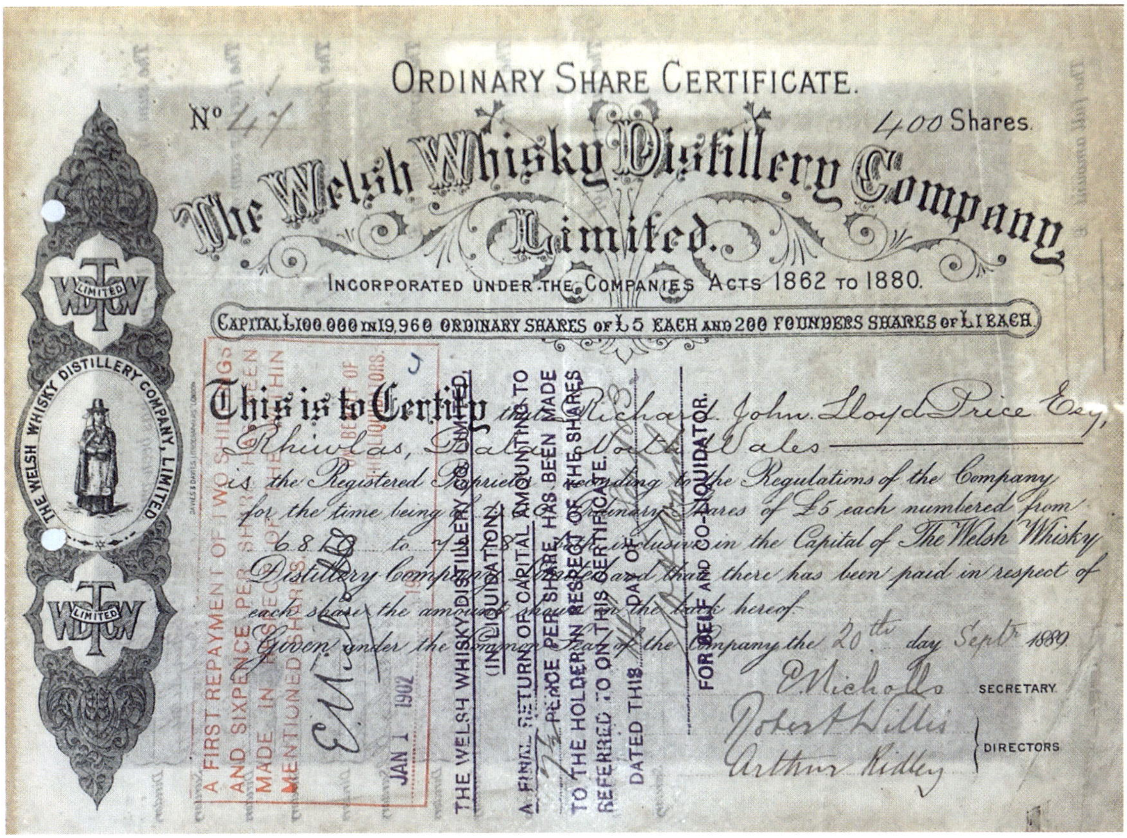
ORDINARY SHARE CERTIFICATE.

No 47 400 Shares.

The Welsh Whisky Distillery Company Limited.

Incorporated under the Companies Acts 1862 to 1880.

Capital £100,000 in 19,960 Ordinary Shares of £5 each and 200 Founders Shares of £1 each.

This is to Certify that Richard John Lloyd Price Esq, Rhiwlas, Bala, North Wales is the Registered Proprietor according to the Regulations of the Company for the time being of [illegible] Ordinary Shares of £5 each numbered from 68[illegible] to [illegible] inclusive in the Capital of The Welsh Whisky Distillery Company Limited and that there has been paid in respect of each share the amount shown in the back hereof.

Given under the Common Seal of the Company the 20th day Septr 1889.

E. Nicholls SECRETARY

Robert Willis, Arthur Ridley DIRECTORS

The Welsh Whisky Distillery Company, Limited

A first repayment of two shillings and sixpence per share has been made in respect of the within mentioned shares.

Jan 1 1902

The Welsh Whisky Distillery Co. Limited (in liquidation).

A final return of capital amounting to [illegible] pence per share has been made to the holder in respect of the shares referred to on this certificate. Dated this [illegible] day of [illegible]

For self and co-liquidator.

ance Union in South Wales, founded by the poet Sarah Jane Rees, scored one success after another. The drinks industry collapsed like a house of cards. Frongoch Distillery had no choice but to close its books in 1903.

End of story? Far from it.

During the First World War, German prisoners of war were temporarily housed in the empty distillery before being transferred to other camps in England. But it was not until 1916 that the entire barbed-wire infrastructure was used as a prison: in April of that year, the Easter Rising against British rule broke out in Ireland, but was crushed after a bloody conflict. One thousand eight hundred Irish prisoners were taken to Frongoch and imprisoned in the distillery. One of them was Michael Collins. He would stay there until December of that year.

This gave him time to grow as 'the leader'. The prisoners were 'guarded' by predominantly Welsh soldiers, some of whom were sympathetic to the ideas of the Irish rebels. As a result, the atmosphere quickly became pleasant and sloppy. Collins, however, was able to keep the morale high and turn the lax atmosphere into an almost military discipline. In doing so, he laid the foundations of what would become the IRA. He would eventually be recognised as one of the most significant figures of the Irish Revolution, leading the negotiations that resulted in the Irish Free State. Thirty-four men from Frongoch won seats in the Irish parliament. The prison was later nicknamed the 'University of the Revolution'.

The Frongoch Distillery was later demolished. Today, a local school occupies part of the site. Nearby is a plaque with Irish, Welsh and English text and a stake with the Irish flag.

Nothing else remains of the Frongoch Distillery... except some bottles of the authentic Royal Welsh Whisky. One of these (on loan from its owner, King Charles) is proudly displayed at St Fagans National Museum of History, the surprising open-air museum near Cardiff. Two other bottles were auctioned years ago for around 14,000 pounds. And one bottle, half full, stands in the 'old' Penderyn Distillery in the Brecon Beacons.

On 1 March 2019, St David's Day – celebrating the patron saint of Wales – Penderyn released a reinvention of the Royal Welsh Whisky, a peated malt whisky with a port finish: the new Royal Welsh Whisky.

It certainly tastes good, and there is no doubt that it is 'Welsh'.

But 'Royal'? That's a different matter entirely.

48 Enzyme

ENZYME

WHAT

An enzyme is a protein that guides reactions in a living cell

HOW

It is a catalyst that starts, accelerates and controls biochemical reactions in a cell, but is not modified by these reactions

IMPORTANCE

Enzymes are indispensable during whisky production and the processing of alcohol in our bodies

One of the things that keeps me awake is this: I rarely mentioned 'the enzyme' in my previous whisky books. And it bothers me. You'll say: "Don't worry, man; other whisky books don't elaborate on 'the enzyme' either." You're right, but that's the point! Without enzymes, you and I wouldn't be here! Worse still, without enzymes, there wouldn't be whisky. Can you imagine that?

And there is more! Before I go on about enzymes, let me say this first.

You can't get up in the morning without it being the 'international day' of something or other. I don't know who made it up, but it must be a joker. International Day of the Number Pi, International Day of Parental Abuse, International Day of Tuna, International Day of Megalithic Culture, International Day of Celiac Disease, you name it. For whoever invented the concept, every day must be a fiesta!

Now I ask you: is there an 'International Day of the Enzyme'?

No, there is not!

Just one day, only one, for the most essential player in our existence and our whisky?!

Nada!

Of course, you can answer: "But there is already an International Whisky Day!"

Agreed: the 27th of March, the birthday of Michael Jackson. To be clear, I'm not talking about the performer, but another Michael Jackson who used to say, "I can't dance, and I don't drink Coke." The late Michael was a phenomenon, a walking encyclopaedia of... beer! More than 80 per cent of his brilliant books are about beer and often about Belgian beer, in which he was a specialist. I met him several times and, unfortunately, never shared a whisky with him. But he certainly knew a lot about enzymes.

We have no idea how many chemical reactions are happening in our bodies at any time. Endlessly. Luckily, we don't have to get involved in keeping everything running; otherwise, it would be a mess. The whole chaos is controlled by enzymes. At birth, you got them for free. Digestion, blood pressure, muscles, stools, you name it... enzymes handle it all. And they do the same for animals, plants, micro-organisms, etc.

They also do it incredibly fast. Because they don't participate in the reaction, they don't modify themselves, so that they can jump from one task to another. Ingenious.

Each enzyme has its own function. We don't need to worry about which enzyme does what, but it's good to know that they have their own quirks about temperature and acidity. They also all have cute names you can use as passwords: esterase, peptidase, protease, etc.

'Alpha- or beta-amylase', for example, should be treasured. These fine enzymes, produced during the malting process, ensure that the starch in the barley is converted into fermentable sugars during the brewing process. It is a team effort: alpha-amylase first converts the starch into dextrin (which we cannot use yet), and then beta-amylase takes over for further processing into sugars. In the next stage, enzymes from the yeast convert the sugars into alcohol... the base for our whisky.

And then, many years later, we all raise our glasses and enjoy this drink of the gods together. Delicious!

The suckers... not realising that after drinking, they will have to call on another army of enzymes to get that devilish alcohol out of their bodies!

Enter alcohol hydrogenase (ADH), which converts alcohol into ethanol. This is a failure: ethanol is poisonous and affects the organs. However, aldehyde dehydrogenase (ALDH) comes to the rescue, converting the ethanol into acetic acid, which the body can break down into water and carbon dioxide. Oof... all for free.

So, always remember what enzymes have done for you!

But... sigh... I don't think we'll ever see the International Day of the Enzyme.

Too bad that Heinz Hermann Polzer is no more. This poet, singer and songwriter lived in Holland and was a master of the Dutch language. If he were still around, he would undoubtedly be singing the praises of enzymes, just as he did in the 1980s for turnips, chicory, salsify and leeks – four vegetables that were unusual in the Netherlands at the time.

He sang, in gospel style, to a society "that could only be saved by these forgotten vegetables":

Dirt and decay and terror in the streets
Turnips and chicory, salsify and leeks
Pop idiots and football fans
Turnips and chicory, salsify and leeks.

He penned and sang twelve stanzas, and within three weeks, turnips, chicory, salsify, and leeks were on sale in every town in the Netherlands. The demand for these once-unusual vegetables outstripped supply, a testament to the power of Polzer's words and their ability to shape public opinion.

Perhaps one day the 'enzyme' will get help from another language virtuoso.

Heinz Hermann Polzer, who performed under the stage name of 'Drs P', was a Swiss national who had studied economics in the Netherlands.

So, you see, a Swiss man can also become a virtuoso of the Dutch language.

Just as Michael Jackson from Beer Country became a whisky virtuoso.

49 Whisky as a weapon

WHISKY AS A WEAPON

WHAT
US and Europe bickering over economic problems

SOLUTION
Threatening to wield a powerful weapon

WEAPON
Whisky

Imagine it is mid-November 2023, and you are sitting by the window. It's raining cats and dogs. The wind is blowing like crazy. The sky is dark; the streets are grey and empty. Even your dog refuses to go out for his necessary walk in this awful weather. And you sit staring into the distance. The best thing you can do is pour yourself a wee dram. In your year-long quest for the best whisky, you've also discovered several tasty bourbons that have earned a place in the queue of your favourite bottles.

You pour yourself a 'wee' Maker's Mark, let it waltz in your mouth for a while and swallow. Ahhhh... nice. A little colour appears in your day... but then you open the newspaper, and your eye accidentally catches a small article with the ominous title: 'From 1 January 2024: prices of all US whiskies will increase by half, due to a new 50 per cent tax'.

And you thought the day couldn't get any worse!

No, this is not a dark dream, but a harsh reality. It has been in the air for a while, but Ursula von der Leyen, President of the European Commission, has confirmed it.

What have we done wrong?

Nothing; in fact, it is not the first time that whisky has been used to overturn decisions made by other countries. It's all the fault of 'steel and aluminium'. And Donald Trump.

In 2018, things did not go well between the then-president and the EU (and the whole world) on several trade issues. The hottest issue was steel and aluminium. That year, Trump imposed strict rules that were unacceptable to the EU. In response, Europe immediately slapped a 25% tax on all imported US whiskey.

That set the ball rolling.

The following year, the US also imposed a 25% tax on all Scotch and Irish whiskey, leading to Europe imposing 25% on all US rum, vodka, and brandy by 2020. Then, you guessed it, the US introduced a 25% tax on, among other things, all cognac from Europe.

The results were clear! Between 2018 and 2020, US whisky exports to Europe fell by almost 30 per cent, a turnover loss of more than a billion dollars. Whisky imports from the UK to America fell by 49 per cent, whereas they had increased by 94 per cent in the ten years before.

And then, in 2022, they agreed to meet. They decided that by the end of 2023, the steel and aluminium issues would be off the table. The tariff game was stopped overnight.

Good news followed soon after: US whisky exports to the EU were up 118 per cent in the first half of 2023, compared with the same period in 2022.

But the US whisky world is not yet at ease. The pressing question is: will everything be OK after 1 January? Are we rid of the steel-aluminium problem? Will we still hear Ursula von der Leyen? Will these Europeans put our whisky out of business?

These questions are not only being asked in Kentucky. Whiskey is produced in and exported from thirty-six states in the US. There are already over 2,600 distilleries in Uncle Sam's country! That's eighty times more than in 2000. Together, they account for a product value of more than five billion dollars, and one-quarter of this is exported. Whisky alone accounts for 62 per cent of all drinks exports.

And what about British whisky? Are they also under fire?

On 31 January 2020, Britain's marriage to Europe ended: Brexit was a fact. Whisky producers watched the ever-declining export figures (and all the other problems) with suspicion. In 2023, exports to the United States were still down 7 per cent, or around £100 million.

But the Scots are hopeful as they look forward to the end of 2024, when the taxes imposed on single malt Scotch whisky in 2019 should be off the table. At the end of the tunnel, a tariff-free trade for Scotch whisky in the US should be waiting for them.

50 Aber Falls Distillery

Compared to 'Llanfairpwllgwyngyllgogerychwyrndrobwllllantysiliogogogoch', the longest place name in Wales, 'Abergwyngregyn' is a piece of cake. Abergwyngregyn means 'where the river with the white shells flows out'. Admit it: it sounds lovely and romantic, but I can understand why this picturesque, historic village's two hundred or so residents preferred to shorten the name to Aber.

Aber is a village with a remarkable history. It sits magnificently at the foot of one of Snowdonia's most beautiful waterfalls: the forty-metre-high Rhaeadr Fawr, wisely shortened to 'Aber Falls' by the locals. The falls feed into a river called the Afon Rhaeadr Fawr, home to unique flora, fauna, and pampered bats. It has been the retreat of choice for Wales's nobility, power and wealth for centuries. It was here that the 'Princes of Wales' came to relax. Until the 13th century, the Prince was always someone who was actually from Wales. The last 'native' Prince of Wales, Llywelyn ap Gruffudd (later rightly called 'Llywelyn the Last'), regularly walked along the Afon Rhaeadr Fawr with his wife, Eleanor of Montfort. This stopped after the English, led by King Edward, murdered him in 1282. Since then, the Prince of Wales has been an Englishman, to the extent that the British royal family can be considered truly English.

ABER FALLS DISTILLERY

WHAT

The first distillery in North Wales in a hundred years

WHERE

In Abergwyngregyn, North Wales

IMPORTANT

Community-oriented distillery

But the landlords remained, and in 1925, the entire village of Abergwyngregyn was for sale.

The villagers put their pennies together and bought it. Aber is now truly 'community owned'; even the recently installed hydroelectric power station belongs to everyone. It makes them strong. And proud.

Along the Afon Rhaeadr Fawr, about three kilometres from the waterfall, a slate factory has been abandoned for years. It was turned into a margarine factory during the war, but all activity fell silent afterwards.

In December 2017, the letters of a new logo were carefully hammered into the neatly whitewashed facade of the old factory building: 'ABER FALLS', with 'DISTYLLFA WHISGI' in small captions underneath.

It instantly became the dream selfie backdrop for the many thousands of visitors who wanted to be immortalised at the first distillery in North Wales for over a hundred years. However, Aber Falls Distillery was doing so well that it had to add a new building a metre and a half in front of the iconic logo. These days, the logo is hard to find.

"But it will be okay," assures Dylan Roberts, the visitor centre manager, "there will be a new logo up front." Meanwhile, he points to the enormous iron dragon lying sleepily by the river.

"Wales has a dragon on its flag," he explains, "but it's not this one. We got this monster from a friend, a CEO working for a Chinese company that wanted to get rid of it."

If that stays the only Chinese influence on Welsh whisky, we can live with it.

Inside the tall building, you'll find everything you'd expect from a well-stocked distillery. Remarkably, there's no one around in the distillery.

"They are studying," Dylan explains, "for the exams tomorrow. All our people are in training. We didn't buy away anyone from the competition, as many new distilleries do. Everyone working here comes from the community and had another job before. They are all retrained."

So, everything at Aber Falls is local. The water is local; the barley is local. The draft, the waste, is donated for free to local farmers as livestock feed.

"In return, they put our logo on their water tank!" laughs Dylan.

Everything is 'community-oriented' and proudly Welsh!

Because that's a sore point.

And that's where things briefly went wrong at Aber Falls.

"We couldn't bottle our whisky locally," explains Dylan, "so we looked for a solution nearby. There was one in Bangor, but that was expensive, and the staff couldn't cope. So we had to move our casks to... England."

Admittedly, that's not far away, but it's outside of Wales.

Meanwhile, that administration had taken a copy of the strict Scottish rules and decided when you can put 'Welsh Whisky' on a whisky label.

Abel Falls was bottled outside Wales, and that is why they couldn't call their whisky 'Welsh'. The problem was quickly rectified, and a new bottling line was built within the Welsh borders.

Aber Falls whisky is once again 100% Welsh.

Even more, the last real Prince of Wales and his wife Eleanor are never far away: at Aber Falls, the pot still is called 'Eleanor', and the spirit bears the name 'Llywelyn'.

If you want to know how to pronounce the latter name correctly, take a sip of good whisky, let the heavenly liquid swirl around your mouth for a while, and then swallow it slowly. And wait a moment.

Enjoy the finish and then exhale slowly: hhhhhhhhh...hhhhhhhh and then say 'hhhhhhhhlywelyn'.

If you do not get it right away, try again. Keep going until you get there.

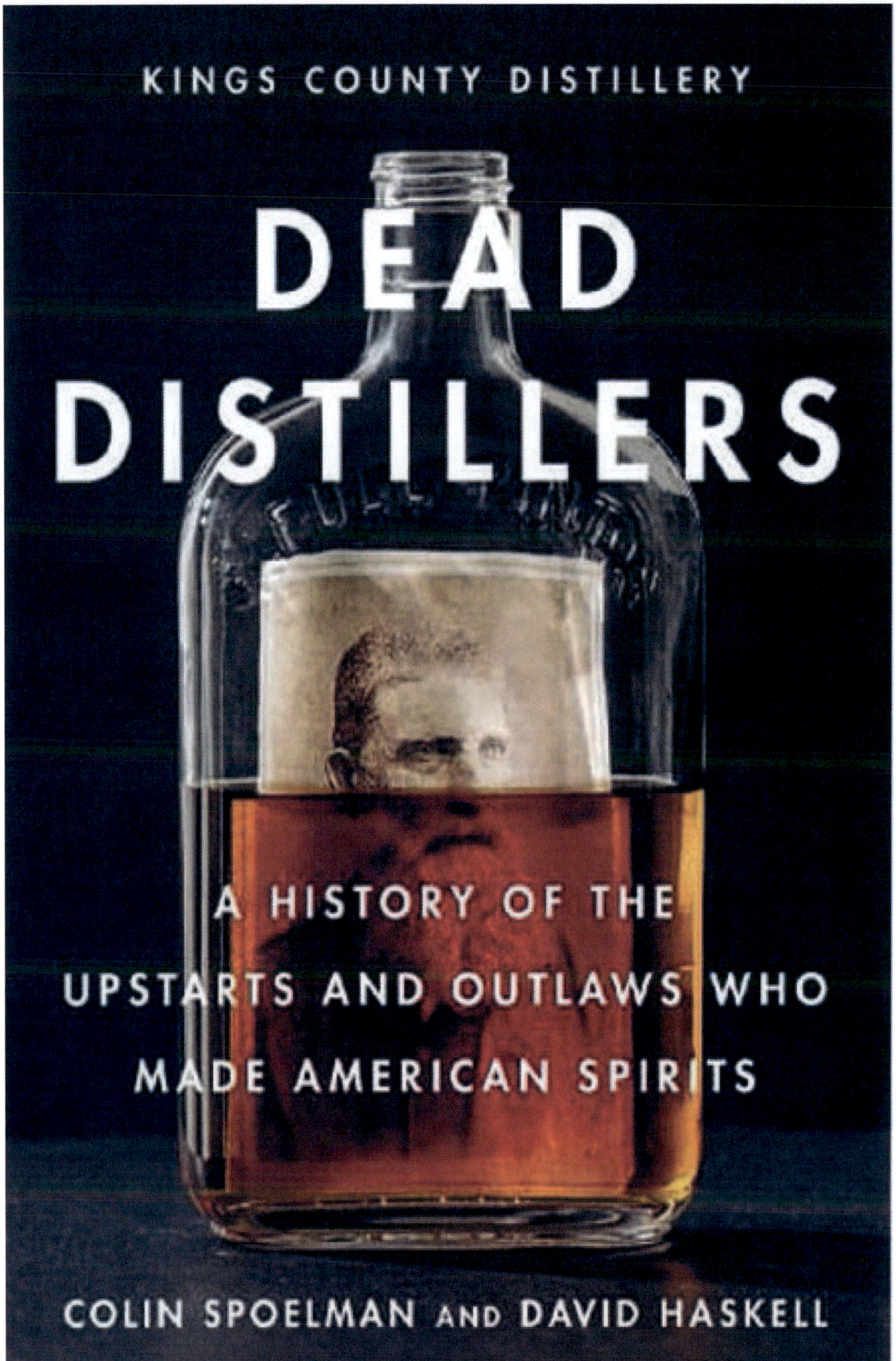
KINGS COUNTY DISTILLERY
DEAD DISTILLERS
A HISTORY OF THE UPSTARTS AND OUTLAWS WHO MADE AMERICAN SPIRITS
COLIN SPOELMAN AND DAVID HASKELL

51 Whisky, love and murder

"The girl was as beautiful as a dewdrop and was known as the city's beauty. Her only fault was a lack of education, but her physical prowess was impeccable. Her hair was pure black but shone blue like a raven, and her eyes were so dark that they sparkled like sparks in a night of impenetrable darkness. Her complexion was as white as the first rays of the sunrise. She was as modest and as pure as the blossoms, buds and flowers on the bushes and branches whose company she kept every day of the spring."

WHISKY, LOVE AND MURDER

CONFESS

You didn't expect to find passionate love and disgusting murder here

PARTICULARLY LOVE

Full of tenderness is rarely found in whisky books

BUT

... it takes us to a strange distillery in New York.

This is a newspaper clipping from the 'Washington Post' at the end of the nineteenth century.

Admit it, there are few whisky books where you come across this kind of lyrical prose.

Good thing you bought this book, isn't it?

To give it away, the girl described above was called Lou Parris. I first came across her name in the book 'Dead Distillers'. The authors, Colin Spoelman and David Haskell, deliberately chose deceased distillers because there are more dead than living by this point. It also indicates their keen business insight: in 2010, they co-founded the Kings County Distillery, the first distillery in New York since the end of Prohibition.

Colin Spoelman was born in Kentucky, the land of bourbon and moonshine. As a child, he noticed how easy it was to get a bottle of whisky from a clandestine distillery. That caught his attention, but he went in a completely different direction: theatre, movie and architecture.

He settled in New York but soon expanded his kitchenette to include a compact still, evidently hidden away, that he used to make his own moonshine. This, of course, violated all the relevant American laws and caused him remorse. He dreamed of owning his own licenced distillery, where he could distil his own bourbon and use his creativity to attain a special place in the whisky world.

His friend David Haskell, a magazine editor but (like Colin) a jack of all trades, was immediately sold on the idea and joined the project.

Today, 14 years later, Kings County's four whiskies make frequent appearances in the press.

These include a young moonshine made from 80 per cent organic corn and 20 per cent malted barley; a three-year-old single malt containing 40 per cent peated Scottish malt; and a unique peated bourbon whiskey made with peat from Aberdeenshire. All distilled in 'real' Scottish stills, no fiddling with columns and dephlegmators.

But they are particularly proud of their 'Bottled-in-Bond Bourbon', which shows courage and creativity, preferring to age some of their bourbons for many years – in Bond – in order to market the oldest bourbons outside Bourbon County.

Oh... sorry, I got sidetracked for a moment... you probably stayed with Lou Parris.

Back to the 'Washington Post'.

You may have missed it, but amid its glorifying prose, the newspaper says, reading between the lines: "Her only flaw was a lack of education".

Surely, the 'Post' should have known better; the reader might think she was a foolish girl, and nothing could be further from the truth. And she would prove it.

One sunny morning in 1894, Lou Parris unsuspectingly walked past a bench where Ralph Redmond was sitting. Ralph, then twenty-one years old, was an accomplished distiller (illegally, of course) and a connoisseur of female beauty. In short, it was love at first sight. Their future was bright and would have been forever, had not father Parris hated lawbreakers, and Ralph Redmond was definitely one of them. Father said 'no way', and the beautiful Lou Parris cried for many days. To comfort her, Papa looked for a replacement and found one in William Johnston, a young man of pleasing personality known in the community as solid and competent. And, like Papa Parris, a teetotaller. Lou pretended to accept the decision and became engaged to the newcomer.

But quietly, she had summed up all the facts and devised a plan: she would send William off in all directions with gimmicks while secretly flirting and frolicking exuberantly with Ralph. (Didn't I say she wasn't stupid?) But William wasn't oblivious either; after a while, he discovered the deception and wanted revenge – not on Lou, but on Ralph. And so he did what is considered the lowest of the

And so he did what is considered the lowest of the low in the whisky world: he went to the IRS and declared Ralph a smuggler. Disgusting!

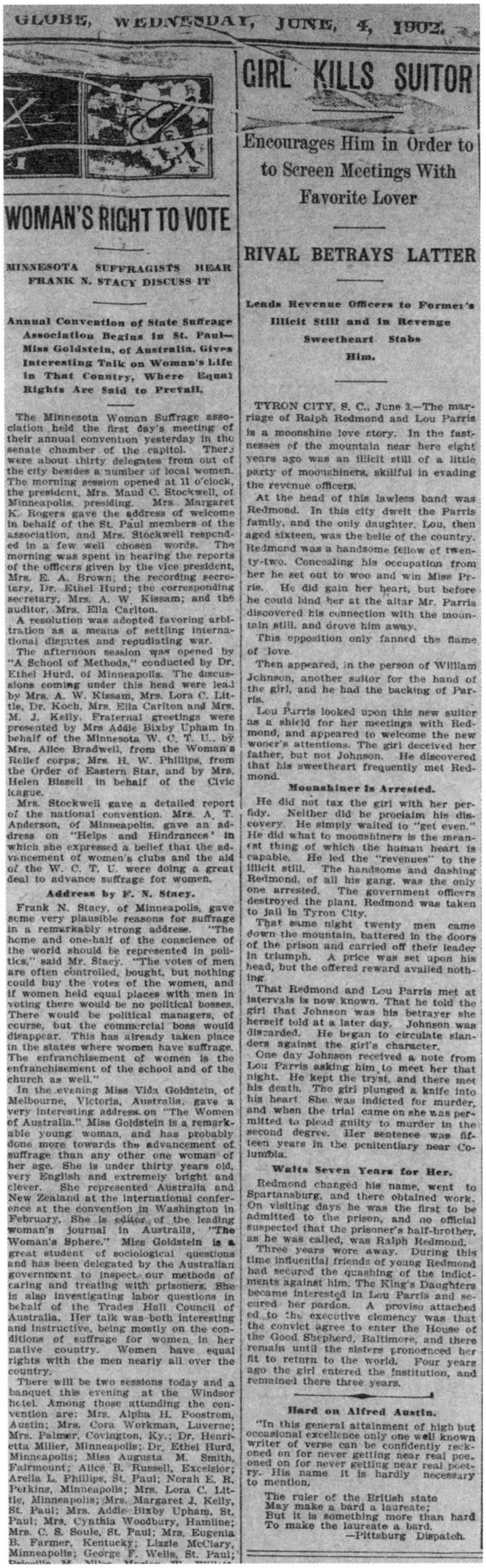

GLOBE, WEDNESDAY, JUNE 4, 1902.

WOMAN'S RIGHT TO VOTE

MINNESOTA SUFFRAGISTS HEAR FRANK N. STACY DISCUSS IT

Annual Convention of State Suffrage Association Begins in St. Paul—Miss Goldstein, of Australia, Gives Interesting Talk on Woman's Life in That Country, Where Equal Rights Are Said to Prevail.

The Minnesota Woman Suffrage association held the first day's meeting of their annual convention yesterday in the senate chamber of the capitol. There were about thirty delegates from out of the city besides a number of local women. The morning session opened at 11 o'clock, the president, Mrs. Maud C. Stockwell, of Minneapolis, presiding. Mrs Margaret K. Rogers gave the address of welcome in behalf of the St. Paul members of the association, and Mrs. Stockwell responded in a few well chosen words. The morning was spent in hearing the reports of the officers given by the vice president, Mrs. E. A. Brown; the recording secretary, Dr. Ethel Hurd; the corresponding secretary, Mrs. A. W. Kissam; and the auditor, Mrs. Ella Carlton.

A resolution was adopted favoring arbitration as a means of settling international disputes and repudiating war.

The afternoon session was opened by "A School of Methods," conducted by Dr. Ethel Hurd, of Minneapolis. The discussions coming under this head were lead by Mrs. A. W. Kissam, Mrs. Lora C. Little, Dr. Koch, Mrs. Ella Carlton and Mrs. M. J. Kelly. Fraternal greetings were presented by Mrs Addie Bixby Upham in behalf of the Minnesota W. C. T. U., by Mrs. Alice Bradwell, from the Woman's Relief corps; Mrs. H. W. Phillips, from the Order of Eastern Star, and by Mrs. Helen Bissell in behalf of the Civic league.

Mrs. Stockwell gave a detailed report of the national convention. Mrs. A. T. Anderson, of Minneapolis, gave an address on "Helps and Hindrances" in which she expressed a belief that the advancement of women's clubs and the aid of the W. C. T. U. were doing a great deal to advance suffrage for women.

Address by F. N. Stacy.

Frank N. Stacy, of Minneapolis, gave some very plausible reasons for suffrage in a remarkably strong address. "The home and one-half of the conscience of the world should be represented in politics," said Mr. Stacy. "The votes of men are often controlled, bought, but nothing could buy the votes of the women, and if women held equal places with men in voting there would be no political bosses. There would be political managers, of course, but the commercial boss would disappear. This has already taken place in the states where women have suffrage. The enfranchisement of women is the enfranchisement of the school and of the church as well."

In the evening Miss Vida Goldstein, of Melbourne, Victoria, Australia, gave a very interesting address on "The Women of Australia." Miss Goldstein is a remarkable young woman, and has probably done more towards the advancement of suffrage than any other one woman of her age. She is under thirty years old, very English and extremely bright and clever. She represented Australia and New Zealand at the international conference at the convention in Washington in February. She is editor of the leading woman's journal in Australia, "The Woman's Sphere." Miss Goldstein is a great student of sociological questions and has been delegated by the Australian government to inspect our methods of caring and treating with prisoners. She is also investigating labor questions in behalf of the Trades Hall Council of Australia. Her talk was both interesting and instructive, being mostly on the conditions of suffrage for women in her native country. Women have equal rights with the men nearly all over the country.

There will be two sessions today and a banquet this evening at the Windsor hotel. Among those attending the convention are: Mrs. Alpha H. Poostrom, Austin; Mrs. Cora Workman, Luverne; Mrs. Palmer, Covington, Ky.; Dr. Henrietta Miller, Minneapolis; Dr. Ethel Hurd, Minneapolis; Miss Augusta M. Smith, Fairmount; Alice B. Russell, Excelsior; Arella L. Phillips, St. Paul; Norah E. R. Perkins, Minneapolis; Mrs. Lora C. Little, Minneapolis; Mrs. Margaret J. Kelly, St. Paul; Mrs. Addie Bixby Upham, St. Paul; Mrs. Cynthia Woodbury, Hamline; Mrs. C. S. Soule, St. Paul; Mrs. Eugenia B. Farmer, Kentucky; Lizzie McClary, Minneapolis; George F. Wells, St. Paul;

GIRL KILLS SUITOR

Encourages Him in Order to to Screen Meetings With Favorite Lover

RIVAL BETRAYS LATTER

Leads Revenue Officers to Former's Illicit Still and in Revenge Sweetheart Stabs Him.

TYRON CITY, S. C., June 3.—The marriage of Ralph Redmond and Lou Parris is a moonshine love story. In the fastnesses of the mountain near here eight years ago was an illicit still of a little party of moonshiners, skillful in evading the revenue officers.

At the head of this lawless band was Redmond. In this city dwelt the Parris family, and the only daughter, Lou, then aged sixteen, was the belle of the country. Redmond was a handsome fellow of twenty-two. Concealing his occupation from her he set out to woo and win Miss Parris. He did gain her heart, but before he could bind her at the altar Mr. Parris discovered his connection with the mountain still, and drove him away.

This opposition only fanned the flame of love.

Then appeared, in the person of William Johnson, another suitor for the hand of the girl, and he had the backing of Parris.

Lou Parris looked upon this new suitor as a shield for her meetings with Redmond, and appeared to welcome the new wooer's attentions. The girl deceived her father, but not Johnson. He discovered that his sweetheart frequently met Redmond.

Moonshiner Is Arrested.

He did not tax the girl with her perfidy. Neither did he proclaim his discovery. He simply waited to "get even." He did what to moonshiners is the meanest thing of which the human heart is capable. He led the "revenues" to the illicit still. The handsome and dashing Redmond, of all his gang, was the only one arrested. The government officers destroyed the plant. Redmond was taken to jail in Tyron City.

That same night twenty men came down the mountain, battered in the doors of the prison and carried off their leader in triumph. A price was set upon his head, but the offered reward availed nothing.

That Redmond and Lou Parris met at intervals is now known. That he told the girl that Johnson was his betrayer she herself told at a later day. Johnson was discarded. He began to circulate slanders against the girl's character.

One day Johnson received a note from Lou Parris asking him to meet her that night. He kept the tryst, and there met his death. The girl plunged a knife into his heart. She was indicted for murder, and when the trial came on she was permitted to plead guilty to murder in the second degree. Her sentence was fifteen years in the penitentiary near Columbia.

Waits Seven Years for Her.

Redmond changed his name, went to Spartansburg, and there obtained work. On visiting days he was the first to be admitted to the prison, and no official suspected that the prisoner's half-brother, as he was called, was Ralph Redmond.

Three years wore away. During this time influential friends of young Redmond had secured the quashing of the indictments against him. The King's Daughters became interested in Lou Parris and secured her pardon. A proviso attached ed to the executive clemency was that the convict agree to enter the House of the Good Shepherd, Baltimore, and there remain until the sisters pronounced her fit to return to the world. Four years ago the girl entered the institution, and remained there three years.

Hard on Alfred Austin.

"In this general attainment of high but occasional excellence only one well known writer of verse can be confidently reckoned on for never getting near real poeoned on for never getting near real poetry. His name it is hardly necessary to mention.

The ruler of the British state
May make a bard a laureate;
But it is something more than hard
To make the laureate a bard.
—Pittsburg Dispatch.

low in the whisky world: he went to the IRS and declared Ralph a smuggler. Disgusting! (But this is still frequently done by jilted lovers and mistresses.) Ralph Redmond was arrested and jailed, but Lou recruited some of his friends, and they managed to free him without much violence (clever, eh?). Ralph temporarily disappeared from the known world, and nobody knew where he was... except Lou, who had devised another plan.

She suggested to William that they find somewhere private and play around in a very romantic and secluded place. Happy to have her all to himself, William fell into the trap with his eyes wide open. While he was still trying to undo the top button of her blouse, she pulled out a razor-sharp knife from under her left garter and plunged it straight into his heart. (Proving once again that she also knew about the anatomy of the human body. Stupid woman? Forget it.)

Lou confessed to the murder and ended up in prison, but due to her exemplary behaviour and perhaps her beautiful eyes, the judges decided on her early release.

In 1902, she married Ralph Redmond, and the happy couple built their love nest in Baltimore, Maryland.

This cruel and harsh story ends in beauty, for everyone except William Johnston.

And as for the whisky world of the time, Ralph took a job with the tram company and never produced a drop of illegal whisky again.

Oh well, all good things must come to an end.

LAPHROAIG
ESTABLISHED
ISLAY 1815 MALT
BY APPOINTMENT TO HRH THE PRINCE OF WALES,
DISTILLER AND SUPPLIER OF SINGLE MALT SCOTCH WHISKY,
D. JOHNSTON & CO., (LAPHROAIG) ISLE OF ISLAY
LAPHROAIG®
ISLAY SINGLE MALT
SCOTCH WHISKY
10
Years Old
The most richly flavoured of
all Scotch whiskies
ESTABLISHED 1815
DISTILLED AND BOTTLED IN SCOTLAND BY D. JOHNSTON & CO.,
LAPHROAIG DISTILLERY, ISLE OF ISLAY
40% vol
LAPHROAIG DISTILLERY
ESTABLISHED 1815
ARE YOU A FRIEND OF LAPHROAIG?
See Inside for Details
Distilled on the remote island
of Islay off the West coast
of Scotland, Laphroaig is the
most richly flavoured of all
Scotch whiskies

52 Pot ale

One day in June 1847, a shockwave went through Laphroaig, the Islay distillery founded in 1815 by brothers Alexander and Donald Johnston.

We don't know exactly how it happened, but on that day, Donald Johnston was found in a cask of pot ale. As you can probably guess, he was dead. Not the first time it had happened. Admiral Nelson had also been immersed in a barrel of alcohol, but he was dead before he went in; Donald wasn't.

Another difference is that this pot ale contained very little alcohol, and the barrel was much bigger. But when it came down to it, that mattered very little.

Anyway, we need to discuss 'pot ale' (also called burned ale) and 'spent lees'. If you fill the wash still with, say, 15,000 litres of wash, you will get about 5,000 litres of low wines from one distillation. So you are left with 10,000 litres of pot ale, waste! That's a lot.

On a hot day on Islay (just kidding), a vat like that might invite you to jump in for a swim. Did Donald take a dip? I don't think so: pot ale is pale yellow, with grain flakes and other grits floating around in it, and it doesn't smell good, a bit burnt.

And it's certainly not because of the alcohol: barely 0.1 per cent.

So what do we do with this mess? Throw it away? No. In some places, pot ale is dumped into the sea (albeit under supervision), but pot ale also contains remnants of yeast, nutritious carbohydrates and proteins, which shouldn't be wasted. This pot ale can be put to better use: food for quadrupeds. The leading candidates are horses, cattle and pigs.

The problem is that more than 95 per cent of pot ale is water. It's not very nutritious in that form, believe me. But if we let the water evaporate, we get a more solid mixture: pot ale syrup, half of which is still water. Pigs and cows love it. Horses get an extra treat: pot ale syrup is mixed with 'draft' (the waste from the barley at the beginning of the production process, when we extract the sugar from the grain).

However, we have not yet considered one of the most fundamental characteristics of pot ale: heat. We hope for Donald Johnston's sake that he did not end up in a kettle of fresh pot ale, because the stuff is boiling. Too hot to be any good for swimming in.

It costs a lot of money to heat the still to this point. To give you an idea, to heat 15,000 litres of wash from ninety to a hundred degrees, you have to fire it for an extra half an hour.

We want that heat back. Damn it.

POT ALE

WHAT
By-product of the distilling process

WHEN
At the end of the first distillation

USE
In animal feed

And we get it. We immediately chase the pot ale through a heat exchanger: we send the hot pot ale down pipes around which cold water flows. The pot ale heats the water to about seventy degrees. The pot ale cools down, but we don't care. This simple trick will save us a lot of pounds when we use that water later. Money, money, money.

After the second distillation, in the spirit still, the 'waste' goes the same route, but it gets a different name now: 'spent lees'. It still contains a lot of residue from the grains used, allowing it to be processed into animal feed as well.

Nothing is lost in the distillery.

The Laphroaig Distillery ↓

In gin distilleries, the cloudy stuff that comes out of the column still as waste is called 'spent wash'. Like pot ale, it is over 90 per cent water. When 'the swill is too thin', it literally means that there's not enough nutritious stuff in it.

I recently met Eric Lootens at the Filliers Distillery. He runs a farm nearby and has just come to collect the swill for his cows. I jokingly asked him, "What do you think of the swill? Not too thin?" He looked at me pitifully.

"Sir," he said, "the swill is ALWAYS too thin."

And he is a connoisseur. You see... these are certainties.

The swill is always too thin. 'All whiskies are small whiskies'. A bottle of whisky is too much for one but not enough for two. And so on.

There are few exact sciences where axioms can be captured in so few simple words.

Beautiful nonetheless.

53 White Dog

If you look closely at the map of Great Britain, you will notice a small dot called the Isle of Man in the Irish Sea between England and Ireland. The island is not part of the United Kingdom, nor is it part of the European Union. It is part of the 'British Crown Dependencies', which could also be referred to as 'a little island garden owned by the monarch'. Mann (as it is sometimes written) is best known for its tailless cats and its lack of speed limits (except in built-up areas). Hence the many bloodstained 'motor races'.

But more interesting, the Isle of Man is the birthplace of Manx Whisky. This distillate was created in the sixties by the Kella Distillery. They bought Scotch malt whisky and expertly re-distilled the matured malt. The result was a colourless but obviously flavourful new spirit, which was immediately bottled. Manx Whisky was an instant success and was exported to England, too. That was against the rules of the Scotch Whisky Association (SWA). After a lengthy legal battle, Kella was forced to change the name to Manx Spirit.

Right on time, because a Manx Whisky Company has since been created, which will abide by the three-year rule and launch a Manx Whisky in 2024.

Because... once again, and now I'm getting angry, whisky must mature for at least three years in a wooden cask. And with that, all is said. It is clearly stated in EU Regulation 2008/110 and reiterated in its updated version, EU Regulation 2019/787. Major whisky countries outside Europe also adhere to this, except Australia (where it is only two years) and the United States, where it only applies to Straight Bourbon (two years) and Bottled in Bond (four years).

WHITE DOG

WHAT

White Dog is a 'new spirit', a 'whisky distillate' that has not matured in a cask

WHERE

White Dog, sold in bottles, is mainly an American phenomenon but is also popping up in other countries

SYNONYMS

White Whisky, Baby Whisky, Moonshine, White Mule, Clearic Spike and a few more...

We owe this three-year requirement to David Lloyd George, the British Minister of Munitions and War during the First World War. From him, we have the 1915 exclamation: "We have to fight Germany, Austria and Alcohol, and as far as I can see, Alcohol is the greatest of these deadly enemies".

And he immediately introduced a three-year maturation period for whisky (initially two, but then increased to three).

David Lloyd George was not only a chronic womaniser with a trained eye for pretty secretaries, he was also a teetotaller. But his dislike of whisky was not the main reason for his Immature Spirits Act of 1915! Excessive drinking among the working class (and the absenteeism that went with it) was causing munitions production to lag, and that had to change. And so it has remained to this day. However, we drink a lot less now – fortunately.

This way, we finally discovered that 70 per cent of all the goodness in our whisky comes from the cask. (Even before 1915, several distilleries had long known this and used casks to mature their whiskies.)

Thank goodness... but come on, enough jubilation; we must move on.

The question now is: was Manx Spirit really the forerunner of this whole 'pale whisky' thing? That nasty habit started in America about two decades ago with White Dog.

They would pour day-old, colourless new spirit into bottles and sell it under the most seductive names: Death's Door, Popcorn Sutton, Glen Thunder, Dark Corner, Dead Guy, Georgia Moon, Ole Smoky Blue Flame, Platte Valley Moonshine, White Lightning, etc.

Even Buffalo Trace, among its other laudable whiskies, has launched a 'Buffalo Trace White Dog', 62.5% ABV and 'guaranteed not a day in a barrel' and 'gin clear'.

What more could you want?

I don't know; I haven't tasted a single white whisky yet. However, the inevitable flavour notes make me hesitant: raw, explosive, slightly spicy, a little sweet, grainy, vodka-like, reminiscent of turpentine...

However, Manx Spirits have a much more positive press: during distillation, the 'head' is cut off to retain as much of the malt's congeners as possible, which is why connoisseurs speak of a "smooth spirit with a nice fruit flavour and no trace of peat". The latter is just as well, as peat cutting is banned on the Isle of Man.

Finally, a word of advice: never confuse 'White Dog' with 'White Horse'. Anyone who remembers the brilliant campaigns for this Scottish blend in the 1970s will know that 'you can take a White Horse anywhere'... In the middle of an endless Scottish landscape, or in a romantic bathroom with an equally romantic lady...

Always with a white horse. Everywhere.

I'd be more careful with a white dog.

[5 & 6 Geo. 5.] *Immature Spirits (Restriction) Act*, 1915. [Ch. **46.**]

CHAPTER 46.

An Act to restrict the Supply and Sale of Immature Spirits. [19th May 1915.] A.D. 1915.

BE it enacted by the King's most Excellent Majesty, by and with the advice and consent of the Lords Spiritual and Temporal, and Commons, in this present Parliament assembled, and by the authority of the same, as follows:

1.—(1) No British or foreign spirits shall be delivered for home consumption unless they have been warehoused for a period of at least three years: *Restriction on delivery for the purposes of home consumption of immature spirits.*

Provided that—

(*a*) this restriction shall not apply to spirits delivered for purposes for which they may for the time being be delivered free of duty or to mixtures, compounds or preparations which have been charged to duty in respect of the spirit contained in them or used in their preparation or manufacture; and

(*b*) subject to the payment of such duties (if any) as Parliament may determine, and to compliance with such conditions as the Commissioners of Customs and Excise may impose, this restriction shall not apply—

(i) to spirits delivered to a licensed rectifier, to a manufacturing chemist, or to a manufacturer of perfumes, for use in their manufactures, or to other persons licensed by the Commissioners of Customs and Excise; or

(ii) to spirits delivered for scientific purposes; or

(iii) to imported Geneva and perfumed spirits and foreign liqueurs; and

(*c*) subject to the payment of such duties (if any) as Parliament may determine and to compliance with such conditions as the Commissioners of Customs

1

← The Immature Spirits Act
Buffalo Trace →

NATIONAL
HISTORIC
LANDMARK
DISTILLERY
499
12 02 09

BUFFALO TRAC
DISTILLERY
BOURBON WHISKEY

54 Tasting blind

In my 'previous life' as a copywriter, I was asked by a dairy company to write a brochure about their yoghurts. This came in handy, since I had decided never to drink more whisky than I consumed yoghurt on any given day, I had become a regular yoghurt eater over the years. I visited the factory for a whole day to familiarise myself. I discovered that their strawberry yoghurt (my favourite because of its deep strawberry flavour) was coloured with... beetroot juice. Fortunately, there were always pieces of strawberry floating in it. But I still wondered: had I been tricked? Or should I be happy with the beetroot juice?

TASTING BLIND

WHAT
Tasting without looking

HOW
By using blue tasting-glasses

REASON
To avoid the colour of the whisky influencing your taste

Any experienced whisky lover knows you must use all your senses when tasting. We only have about five of them, and compared to other species of the same creation, we don't have many reasons to indulge them to excess. Therefore, we need to use our senses to the full. Smell and taste are important; they work often together and produce acceptable results.

The sense of hearing is often forgotten: the pop of the cork triggers half your salivary glands (think Pavlov and his classic conditioning).

Whisky books do not devote much space to vision: look at the 'legs sliding slowly down the glass after swirling'. Or not being there at all. And that's about it. The colour... yes, we know caramel is allowed at E150, so we connoisseurs don't fall for it!

However, some unscrupulous people will try to trick you: they will offer you the whisky to taste in a blue glass. This is supposed to prevent you from being influenced by the whisky's colour. OK, that's not punitive, but the surprising fact is that the use of a coloured glass actually influences the taster's taste buds.

This was proved by a series of tests at the University of Portsmouth in England. Subjects were served a series of identical snacks, each time on a different coloured plate, lying that "the snacks were served with minor changes to the recipe."

The result: the snacks on the red plates were rated the least tasty, while those on the blue plates were rated good but far too salty. Obvious, right?

Even more so, researchers at Oxford University discovered that we only use 2 per cent of our cerebral cortex when tasting. The cerebral cortex is the part of the brain that analyses and interprets all the information we receive from our senses. Only 2 per cent.

But… this is astonishing: the signals the brain receives from our eyes activate more than half of the cerebral cortex. More than half!

And we call it 'blind' tasting?

Around 1900, Albert Henri Munsell, an American painter and inventor, developed a particular colour chart based not only on the properties of a colour, but also on the reactions of test persons when they saw that specific colour. He was the first to include this relationship in his charts.

The United States Department of Agriculture still uses his colour charts for fruit and vegetables. It has also been used in dentistry, breweries, cosmetics, and even to assess semi-baked bread and crisps.

Have you ever wondered why the same Easter eggs are often wrapped in different coloured paper? We know from Munsell's results that pink is sweet, green is salt, orange is pepper and yellow is sour.

And blue?

Blue is not tasty. Blue is not edible. Give me three blue dishes you can order in a restaurant. Blue is disgusting. And now I'm weighing my words!

So forget about those idiotic blue glasses; let your whisky have colour. It doesn't matter if that colour has been tinted a bit. What matters is the overall experience and the mood the whisky puts you in.

Because there's one sense that rarely comes into play (but I'm not sure it's a 'sense'): our imagination.

Try the test with your next whisky! Close your eyes and imagine yourself in the Highlands, huddled by a crackling fire overlooking the ever-changing mountains and a vast lake. Taste your dram.

Keep your eyes closed. Imagine you are sitting in a small attic room, looking out at a bleak sky behind the dilapidated chimneys of a paint factory that closed in 1942.

Taste that same dram... I am sorry to do this to you.

Johann Wolfgang von Goethe said it, back in 1773: "Experience teaches us that every colour creates a certain mood and every mood creates an experience."

I don't know if he was talking about whisky, but I couldn't have said it any better.

55 Whisky (un)certainties

WHISKY (UN)CERTAINTIES

A QUOTE

"There is only one certainty in this world: nothing is certain!"

AUTHOR

No clue

OUR VIEW

One thing is certain in the world of whisky

Are you familiar with the concept of 'hiraeth'?

'Hiraeth' is Welsh, that impossible language with those many, many almost-unpronounceable words. You won't find an acceptable translation for 'hiraeth' in any of our neighbouring languages. Some dictionaries make a commendable attempt and offer 'nostalgia' or 'homesickness' as a solution... but these words fall short of capturing its true essence.

Hiraeth is an overwhelming feeling of pent-up sadness, together with a longing for a place you've never been, a kind of heightened spiritual homesickness. You either have hiraeth, or you don't. I don't know if it's a typically Welsh affliction, but I suspect that Evan Williams, who was born in Dale – on the south-western tip of Wales – experienced rather a lot of this hiraeth.

In 1780, he left Wales and set off for America, which was unknown territory to him. Twenty-five years old at the time, he had set up a small distillery in Wales, but his drink wasn't exactly a hit.

All the excellent whisky and history books will tell you the whole story.

He settled in Louisville, Kentucky, situated on the Ohio River. The river makes some crazy bends here, suddenly dropping metres, and that's where the Ohio Falls were formed. Goods brought in by boat would be transferred to wagons before the falls, carried past the falls and reloaded to another ship. Evan soon realised that this had to be organised, and he became Kentucky's first harbourmaster. He had also noticed from the start that there was a lot of grain in the region, and a lot of corn too, more than was needed locally – and he knew just what to do with it. In 1783, Evan set up a distillery. We know that Louisville had a distillery at that time with three stills: two of 500 litres and one of 100 litres. This is where the first 'Evan Williams Whiskey' is said to have been made.

In addition to his whisky work, he was also a builder and is credited with building not only the first brick house in Louisville, but also the first jail and the first courthouse. His fame *automatically* led him into local politics.

In other words, Evan Williams became a man of distinction. The same cannot be said for his whisky. Of course, we never tasted it ourselves, but we can deduce from casual 'tasting notes' that the drink was unpalatable.

To be clear, his Evan Williams whisky has nothing to do with the famous Evan Williams whisky that is still produced today at the Heaven Hill Distillery, which is one of the best-selling American whiskies.

Anyway, where this distillery once stood in Louisville, a large plaque reads: "Evan Williams, a native of Wales, came to Kentucky about 1780, where he built his distillery on the banks of the Ohio River in 1783. He distilled whiskey from corn grown on the east side of what is now 5th Street. It is said that this was the first commercial distillery in Kentucky."

"It is said..." Can you feel the doubt in those words? Well, you're right.

The 'Filson Historical Society' was founded in Louisville in 1884 by amateurs who conducted historical research and collected millions of historical documents relating to the city. They claim to be able to prove that Evan Williams arrived in Louisville in May 1794, 11 years after the first distillery was established. That means we can forget about 'the first commercial distillery in Kentucky' as far as Williams is concerned – unless, of course, the society is wrong.

As you can see, there are no more certainties.

While we're at it, let's solve this Bushmills problem right now, shall we?

Every Bushmills bottle triumphantly proclaims: "Ireland's oldest whiskey distillery. Original grant to distil in 1608."

We know that the first written mention of the distillery dates from 1743 when a gang of smugglers were plying their trade here, and that Old Bushmills was not granted a licence until 1784.

Once again, we turn to Alfred Barnard (author of 'The Whisky Distilleries of the United Kingdom'). He visited The Bushmills Old Distillery Company in 1886.

"The company has recently increased the capacity of their old pot stills," he wrote, "and they have installed electric light in their premises, which has a very charming effect. This clearly shows that they are ready for all modern inventions."

No wonder, since the business had been entirely destroyed by fire two years

earlier, and everything had been quickly rebuilt. However, Barnard did not mention 1608. In his book we discover that of the twenty-eight distilleries Barnard visited, only Tullamore and Midleton still exist; and they only date back to the nineteenth century.

So we take 'Ireland's Oldest Whiskey Distillery' to be true. We concur.

But let's address that '1608'!

Now we'll call on Sir Thomas Phillips.

Figuratively speaking, since he suffered a fatal heart attack in 1636. He was seventy-six at the time. He earned his living as a mercenary, fighting in various European countries and in Africa. For his services (particularly against the French), he was knighted in 1607 and given 1,200 acres of land in Limavady, a town not far from Bushmills. In addition, King James VI of Scotland (who was also James I of England) granted him a licence in 1608 to distil "by himselfe or his servauntes aquavite, usquabagh and aqua composita".

It is this 'grant' that Bushmills refers to on every bottle.

But Sir Thomas Phillips, as far as we know, has nothing to do with Bushmills. We don't even know if he ever owned a distillery and made use of his licence. A certain John Alexander established the Limavady Distillery on this site, but that was in 1750, and this John Alexander had nothing to do with either Phillips or Bushmills.

So you can see why we find 'Original grant to distil 1608' on a bottle of Bushmills to be very uncertain.

We could go on.

Was Edradour really the smallest distillery in Scotland? If not, who is? Are there 34 different whiskies in Johnny Walker Black Label? Absolutely, or is it 18? Was Highland Park founded in 1887, as they claim, or in 1825? Does adding a few drops of water to your whisky make it any better? And... No, stop.

Sorry to drag you into all my uncertainties and burden you with my doubts on this beautiful day.

To make up for it: there is one certainty in the whisky world.

Ask two people (let's call them A and B for convenience) to taste an unfamiliar whisky. If A claims this whisky is delicious, while B insists that that it's beneath contempt, they are both right.

One hundred per cent certain, it would be terrible if we all liked the same whisky.

THE SCOTCH MALT WHISKY SOCIETY
MAVERICK
SINGLE MALT SCOTCH WHISKY
YEARS 12 AGED
70CL℮

56 Samuel Maverick and the SMWS

Spring of 1836.

The Texas War of Independence is raging in San Antonio, Texas. The so-called 'Texan rebels' are fighting for their independence from Mexico. A few hundred Texans take refuge in a Catholic mission building, the world-famous Alamo. Among them were the equally world-famous Davy Crockett and the much lesser-known Samuel Maverick.

On 23 February 1836, the Mexican general López de Santa Anna attacks the mission. The trapped Texans have no chance against the general's 1,500 soldiers, but they decide to fight to the last man. Samuel Maverick manages to escape during the night and calls for help. But before it arrives, the rebels run out of ammunition and are overpowered and killed. Samuel Maverick, the only survivor, would play an essential role in independent Texas.

SAMUEL MAVERICK AND THE SMWS

WHO

Samuel Maverick

AND

SMWS stands for Scotch Malt Whisky Society

TOGETHER

They share the Maverick Syndrome

Just a few hundred yards from the Alamo and on the site of the Maverick family's home, Maverick Distilling now distils Maverick Whiskey, a bourbon and rye whiskey. Run by a descendant of the legendary Samuel Maverick, the distillery is housed in an impressive building that once served as a bank.

Samuel Maverick may well have walked around here. No ordinary man, he came from quite a wealthy family, as evidenced by his status as a slaveholder. Among other things, he was a lawyer, made a political splash and owned an impressive amount of property. He was undoubtedly a man of distinction; although he was imprisoned for a time, he later became mayor of San Antonio. These things often go hand in hand.

But he is best remembered as a landowner and rancher. He once owned a herd of more than four hundred cattle, and that's where the real Maverick emerges. Against all Wild West customs, he refused to have his cattle branded. It hurts the animals, and he didn't want that. But in those days, unbranded animals automatically became the property of the first person to catch them (according to unwritten law). Opponents thought he was trying to get hold of all unbranded animals, but that was far from his intention: he was only trying to be 'contrary' – doing what others wouldn't.

And so the word 'maverick' found its way into all the English dictionaries. One definition reads: "Maverick: a person who demonstrates independence of thought and action, especially by refusing to conform to the policies of a group to which he or she belongs."

While Maverick whisky is a coveted delicacy in America, a Maverick whisky suddenly appeared on the market in Scotland in 2023. 'On the market' needs to be corrected, as only members of the SMWS can buy one. SMWS stands for 'Scotch Malt Whisky Society', the world's largest whisky club and independent bottler. The club was founded in 1983, so the Maverick bottle was produced to celebrate the club's 40th anniversary. You don't have to look far to find out why they chose 'Maverick': Phillip (Pip) Hills, the founder of the SMWS, is as much a contrarian as Samuel, whom we met at the Alamo.

Forty years ago, the Scotch whisky world was in big trouble: several distilleries had gone out of business, leading to the accumulation of a 'whisky loch', a lake of unsold (mostly blended) whisky. Moreover, there was very little interest in single malts overall, let alone cask-strength bottled single cask whiskies.

When Pip Hills announced in the late 1970s that he would buy casks of malt whisky and bottle it at cask strength, everyone thought he was joking. But it soon turned out that his anti-establishment thinking wasn't so crazy after all. He convinced a few friends, and they bought a Glenfarclas cask together. This club of friends constantly expanded, as did the number of casks they purchased. This would earn him the nickname 'Maverick Pip' – hence the name of the exclusive celebratory bottle.

As external demand for their bottlings grew, they spun off SMWS in 1983. At the end of 2023, the club has nearly 40,000 members, owns a cellar of 17,000 casks from 150 distilleries and sold more than 200,000 bottles in 2022. Its primary markets are obviously the UK and Europe, but Taiwan, Korea, Malaysia, China and Australia are also in the top ten.

The SMWS bottles are a sight to behold: neat labels with expertly penned flavour notes right on the front of the bottle. You'll need them, too, because you won't find the distillery's name anywhere! Instead, they use a 'secret' number and a coloured band.

The number code consists of two parts, separated by a full stop. The first part refers to the distillery and the second indicates how many casks from that distillery have ever been bottled by the SMWS. The colour code reflects the flavour of the whisky: bright green is 'full-peated', purple is 'sweet and spicy', and orange-yellow is 'spicy and dry'. A handy colour chart is readily available.

Even the 'secret' number code is not as secret as you might think: the internet lists them all. Number 1 is, noblesse oblige, Glenfarclas! 14 is Talisker, 17 is Scapa, etc. Some codes will take you to rum and cognac distilleries, as members have been able to buy other distillates for a few years now.

Of course, you have to be a member (or have a friend who is) to taste these unique delights. In addition to the bottlings, the SMWS has several venues and club rooms where members are welcomed with open arms in London, Glasgow and Edinburgh, among other places, as well as numerous partner bars worldwide.

THE 12 FLAVOUR PROFILES OF THE SMWS

THE SCOTCH MALT WHISKY SOCIETY
EST? THE VAULTS, LEITH, SCOTLAND

YOUNG & SPRITELY	SWEET, FRUITY & MELLOW	SWEET & SPICY
Muscle rub Beeswax Bitter lemon Tinned mandarins Menthol Flying saucers Sparkling wine Sour apple sweets Extra strong mints Gummi bears Rhubarb Plum tarts Nettles	*Watermelon Pimms Apricot Turkish Delight Orange Muscat Lemon meringue pie Candied orange slices Rhubarb and custard sweets Lime marmalade Piña colada Apple pie Peach Melba Sherbet*	*Gingerbread Garam masala Hot cross buns Cinnamon Danish Balsamic strawberries Thai sweet chilli crisps Seville orange marmalade Dark chocolate ginger biscuits Fresh oak Spice market Fruit cake Mulled wine Cardamom Star anise*
SPICY & DRY	**DEEP, RICH & DRIED FRUITS**	**OLD & DIGNIFIED**
Clove Tree bark Charred stave Sandalwood Liquorice stick Chilli chocolate Rum and raisin Toasted coconut Nutmeg Peppercorns Pipe tobacco Crème brûlée Pencil shavings	*Rum truffles Treacle toffee Demerara Sherry trifle Black bun Mincemeat pies Salted caramel Sticky toffee pudding Balsamic glaze Cinder toffee Marmalade Burnt toffee Orange peel Prunes*	*Honeycomb Cigar box Scented candles Maple syrup Armagnac Mango Pineapple cubes Dark chocolate orange Polished wood Antique shop Old books Brandy snaps Perfumed pear Apple strudel Lychees*
LIGHT & DELICATE	**JUICY, OAK & VANILLA**	**OILY & COASTAL**
Fresh laundry White pepper Peach Banana chips Lemon drizzle cake Honeydew melon Flower meadows Coconut ice-cream Pine Green tea Blossom Patisserie Breakfast cereal	*Oiled wood Toasted oak Coriander seed Pineapple sorbet Dunnage warehouse Carpenter's workshop Millionaire's shortbread Chocolate-coated cherries Root ginger Banana split Passion-fruit Honeysuckle*	*Tarry ropes Oysters Marmite Olive oil Harbour walls Beach bonfire Salted caramel Barbecued prawns Fish boxes Seaweed Boatyard Driftwood Pebble beach*
LIGHTLY PEATED	**PEATED**	**HEAVILY PEATED**
Garden bonfire Vintage cars Burnt twigs Wood ash Smoked salmon Lapsang Souchong tea Toasted marshmallows Dentist's waiting room Incense Rock pools Sea breeze Parma violets Pata negra	*Lavender smoke Heather moor-burn Bonfire embers Ship's engine room Hospital laundry room Smoky bacon crisps Roast rosemary lamb Perfumed pipe smoke Kippers Clean tar First aid box Phenolic Coal tar soap Herbal smoke*	*Steam train Chimney soot Carbolic Coal sacks Fireman's gloves Smoked mackerel Wood burning stove Euthymol toothpaste Gunpowder Cigar butts Burnt pastries Burning ships Farmyard*

57 Whisky Highball

As I am writing these words on my 84th birthday, I am sitting on my terrace with an excellent whisky (thanks to Ardbeg, and to Martin, who brought the bottle) and reading (thanks to the Internet Archive) 'The Fable of the Bees' by Bernard de Mandeville. Bernard was born in Rotterdam on 15 November 1670 but spent most of his life in England, so he wrote mainly in English. 'The Fable of the Bees' is considered his masterpiece.

It is quiet and sunny today on the outskirts of Ghent. It seems as though my day couldn't get any better – but it's about to improve!

WHISKY HIGHBALL

WHAT

Whisky cocktail

ORIGIN

USA around 1890

INGREDIENTS

Whisky and everything else

I read somewhere that 'The Fable of the Bees' is the first English mention of the word 'gin'. Those who know me are well aware that gin is not my favourite drink, so you can comprehend why I was looking forward to hearing what Bernard de Mandeville had to say about this pseudo-beverage.

You see, he writes:

"Nothing is more destructive, either to the health or to the vigilance and zeal of the poor, than that infamous drink, whose name, derived from the Dutch 'genever', has now, through frequent use and the laconic spirit of the nation, shrunk from a word of medium length to a monosyllable, intoxicating gin, which charms the lazy, the desperate, and the mad of both sexes, and makes the starving fool contemplate his rags and nakedness with stupid indolence, or dilutes his senseless laughter into more lame jokes!"

See... didn't I say?! Well done, Bernard. That deserves another shot of Ardbeg.

But I admit: my aversion to (most) gins is due to my lack of knowledge and understanding. I simply don't understand how someone can work diligently to produce a tincture of (I'm just saying) 28 carefully selected herbs, fruits and peels with their own or bought alcohol, and then – when I want to taste it – ask me to add a cucumber peel. Why didn't he add the cucumber himself? 28 or 29 can only make a little difference!

Sorry, it infuriates me. I just need to calm down...

I admit that my repudiation is much more profound. For example, I don't understand why someone would make a drink and bottle it with the intention of selling it to me, among others. And then blatantly writes that I should pour 5 centilitres of it into a spherical glass, add the peel of a lemon, a bay leaf, a dash of Angostura and 15 centilitres of quinine water (the latter preferably slowly, along a curled iron that I should hold vertically in the middle of the glass). And then a few cubes of ice.

And all this is allowed!

"Do I have anything against cocktails?" you ask.

Where did you get that idea from?

My answer is short: "The word 'cocktail' comes from cockfights. It was customary to sell two drinks after a fight: one with alcohol and a few drops of blood from the losing rooster and another without blood. To make it easier for the drinker, a feather from the tail of the rooster who had lost his life was stuck into the glass with the blood. Cock-tail... cocktail, got it?"

Now, do you understand why I (as an animal lover) do not favour cocktails?

Nor do I enjoy them as a whisky lover, but that doesn't bother me: fortunately, there are only a few idiots who dare to put whisky in a cocktail. I tell you true: whisky cocktails will never be a success; straight whisky is far too good. Full stop.

Let's end this discussion here and now. After all, it is my birthday.

I'll have another Ardbeg. A small one.

So I am sitting on my terrace with an excellent whisky, and I have just been able to vent my bile about gin and cocktails. That's heart-warming. What more does one need?

I start my daily digital newspaper round-up with 'The Scotsman'. In the 'Food&Drink' section, you'll find the latest news on Scotch whisky. That's always fun. Let's take a look.

Title: "Tomorrow, 21 July: Whisky Highball Day 2023!"

Whisky Highball Day... Whisky HIGHBALL Day! And we already had a World Whisky Day in May and, for some reason, an International Whisk(e)y Day in March. Come on.

Look, I could live with that; for me, every day is Whisky Day, but now it is another Whisky Highball Day! You guys! Even on my birthday! That hurts.

Yes, I know what a Whisky Highball is!

I first faced it in Tokyo in 2003. The HIGHBALL was promoted on the bar's sign, which made me curious.

The barman calmly took his time using an axe to carve a perfect tennis ball out of a large block of ice. The ball fitted neatly into a large glass, and the small space around it was filled with Johnnie Walker Black Label and soda. With the first sip, my little brain crumpled painfully from the cold.

So yes, I know what a Whisky Highball is. And I had hoped that this Japanese invention (I thought) would stay there, along with eating raw fish and their pre-warmed musical toilet seats! But no.

Whisky Highball Day... where did they get that idea?

I read in the newspaper that the 'highball' was an American invention in 1890, and that the phenomenon spread worldwide from there. There are several recipes in 'The Scotsman', but it all boils down to the same thing: pour one part whisky and three parts something else, anything, into a tall glass filled with ice. There's nothing wrong with that, except that sometimes my favourite whisky is used to commit this crime. Sometimes that something else is suspiciously different: it could even be three parts... kombucha!

I admit, I had to look it up, but this will save you time. Kombucha is a drink made by adding fresh tea to a group of microorganisms in the form of a thick, gelatinous, shiny membrane called a 'fungus', i.e. a symbiotic culture of bacteria and yeast. The main ingredients are lactic acid, acetic acid and vitamins.

You've probably guessed it: it doesn't sound appetising, so it's very healthy. You won't believe what it's claimed to be good for: it detoxifies, cleanses the glandular system, neutralises uric acid and treats many other ailments.

Now, I put myself in the shoes of an avid kombucha drinker. How must that person feel when he learns that, worldwide, his favourite drink is being mixed with a disgustingly unhealthy liquid called whisky? Indeed, he must be angry. Like me when I hear 'Highball'.

Hey... this could be the start of something new.

It took some research, and I found a kombucha club in Canada, 'Culture Shock Kombucha', in Grand Bend, Ontario, just over the border from the USA. I will definitely contact them.

Together, we can fight the Kombucha Highball to obtain a worldwide ban on this mixture. The next step can be a global ban on the Whisky Highball. Really.

Yes, I know... this is wishful thinking.

And if it doesn't work, please... one day a year: 'World Anti-whisk(e)y-Highball Day'.

On 20 July, my birthday.

It would be nice, wouldn't it?

58 Spirit safe

SPIRIT SAFE

WHAT

Handy tool for separating different types of alcohol

SINCE

1825

If there is one person in the whole history of Scotch whisky that I really feel sorry for, it is Septimus Fox. Maybe it's his own fault, but there's not much he can do about it now, since he's been dead for over a hundred and fifty years. Anyway, you rarely find him mentioned in whisky books, and that's not fair because his invention can still be found in all whisky distilleries today, except for those renegades who have switched to computers for specific controls.

Around 1820, Septimus invented a cabinet to inspect the alcohol produced and separate the unwanted parts before it disappeared into the collection vessel: the prototype of the spirit safe. On every visit to a distillery, everyone admiringly stops at this shiny little cabinet where you can see the distillate flowing beautifully into one of the three jars behind the glass. Little did Septimus know that a few years later, with the introduction of the Excise Act of 1823, his invention would become compulsory in all distilleries. This Excise Act stated that whisky could be distilled on payment of a ten-pound fixed licence fee plus an additional amount per gallon distilled. It was, therefore, essential that, before measuring, the usable alcohol was segregated correctly.

To ensure that this 'modern' device would not change the taste of the whisky, the spirit safe was tested for two years at Port Ellen on Islay before becoming compulsory in all distilleries.

One day, the Creator, after a full day's work, must have told the Angel Gabriel: "Gabby, today I've created a lot of things that can be used to make alcohol. I wonder how long it will take them to discover that!"

When Gabriel pointed out the dangers of alcohol, the Creator surely laughed and revealed that he wouldn't make things easy for humanity. And he immediately created several more types of alcohol, but made only one drinkable: ethanol.

And we are stuck with the resulting problem.

Fortunately, these different alcohols evaporate at different temperatures. First to evaporate is the toxic methanol, also known as wood alcohol, which should be avoided. Next comes ethanol (and that's the good stuff), followed by the heavier ones: propanol, butanol, etc.

The latter has tasty elements, but we must be careful with the tiny particles we dare to include in our final product.

So, we need to separate the ethanol (the heart) from the methanol (the head) and the propanol, etc. (the tail).

And that's what we have the spirit safe for.

This cabinet usually has three jars, from which the flow goes to one of the specific containers. On the top of the safe is a handy little lever to direct the flow of the spout to one of the jars. One jar is for the 'low wines' (in the first distillation run), a second is for the head and tail, and the third catches the ethanol (in the second distillation run). The heads and tails join the new low wines for another run in a subsequent distillation to further break them down.

Of course, the handy spirit safe quickly found its way into the distillation of other spirits, including rum, where a similar process occurs.

Still, there are some notable exceptions. As far as I know, only two whisky distilleries have a spirit safe with four jars instead of three, while the new Filliers distillery in Deinze (Belgium) has just one. They also keep the head and tail separate. Only the tail is sent to the next run. The head, only 0.3 per cent of the total distillate, is processed by third parties into... (!) petrol.

And then there's John Crow Batty.

Let's take a trip to the photogenic Queen of Spain Valley in western Jamaica, home to the Hampden Estate rum distillery. The sprawling farm sits on the edge of a tropical garden where peacocks and other large birds roam. Around 1750, Archibald Sterling bought 1,500 acres of land to establish a sugar cane plantation.

You can still pick up a John Crow Batty bottle `somewhere' in Jamaica. 80% ABV.
Brush your teeth after drinking!

Twenty-five years later, a rum distillery was also up and running.

As in the whisky industry, rum distillation involves separating the 'head' and 'tail' from the 'heart'.

"In the old days," I was told, "it was quite common for some workers to take home a bucket of head and tail in the evening. Illegally, of course, but nobody cared about it because this 'drink' was particularly popular with the people. People attributed all sorts of powers to it.

"You could drink it when you were sick, but also when you were well. It was drunk at every birth, and babies were christened with it. It was also great for massages, disinfection or if you were feeling a little down. The only flaw is that it has a rather unpleasant odour, and its tart, pungent taste takes some getting used to."

This 'rum' is colloquially known as John Crow Batty. On this island, the name John Crow refers to the 'Turkish vulture': a bird of prey with a blood-red head, as if its skin has just been ripped off. By 'batty' they mean the tail end, or arse. Few spirits have a name that immediately renders the tasting notes superfluous.

You can still pick up a John Crow Batty bottle 'somewhere' in Jamaica. 80% ABV.

Brush your teeth after drinking!

59 Wi' usquabae, we'll face the devil!

Dumfries and Galloway is not right at the top of the Scottish whisky tourist list, and that's a shame; it's a beautiful and often forgotten region. From Gretna Green, however, it's only a hop, skip and a jump to the fledgling Annandale Distillery, with Bladnoch Distillery just an hour away. Two good reasons to change your plans.

> WI' USQUABAE, WE'LL FACE THE DEVIL!
>
> WHAT
>
> A verse from 'Tam o' Shanter'
>
> MEANS
>
> With whisky, we can face the devil
>
> POET
>
> Robert Burns

Half an hour from Gretna Green, you can also detour to Caerlaverock Castle. I know: Scotland is full of castles, more than three thousand in fact, and you'll have plenty of opportunities elsewhere. But take note: there is (to my knowledge) only one castle with a triangular floor plan in the whole of Scotland, possibly even the entire UK: Caerlaverock. The magnificent monument dates back to the late 13th century; although it has been dilapidated since the 17th century, it is still very photogenic.

In one of the watchtowers, a long-passed 'vandal' carved his initials into the historic stone: in hand-sized letters, it reads 'R.B.', with the year 1776 underneath.

In fact, the purported vandal was none other than Robert Burns, Scotland's national bard! He was popularly known as 'Robbie Burns', but never used that name himself. He is acclaimed as the most important Scottish poet of all time!

His poem 'Address to a Haggis' is still sung worldwide whenever a haggis is ceremonially cut open: "Fair fa' your honest, sonsie face, Great chieftain o' the puddin'-race..."!

It is a pity that he wrote not in English but in Scots, and in the even more obscure dialect of Ayrshire, where he was born. As a result, it sometimes takes extra effort to discover exactly what he meant.

He was born into a farming family on 25 January 1759, and would spend much of his later life on a farm. Sadly, he only lived to be 37; he died of chronic rheumatic fever, which caused his weak heart to fail. He did, however, have a 'big heart', for he had already succumbed to the charms of a number of 'Scottish 'beauties', several of whom later turned out to be pregnant. But he always immortalised them in one of his masterful ballads. Who wouldn't melt at his unsurpassed love song to Mary Campbell?

She has my heart, she has my hand, by secret Truth and Honor's band:

Till the mortal stroke shall lay me low, I'm thine, my Highland Lassie.

And for all the other girls:

O, my luve is like a red, red rose, that's newly sprung in June.

O, my luve is like a melodie, that's sweetly play'd in tune.

It was later discovered that he had taken this last line from an old Scottish song, but no one makes a fuss about it these days.

But Burns's greatest love was the 'juice of the barley': whisky.

Thanks to him, Scotland's national drink found its way into literature. Not that few knights of the pen shied away from a wee dram, far from it, but many poets seem to have exercised some restraint. For his part, Burns took every opportunity to use his best words – and sometimes even to write away his troubles, because that happened to him, too, even with whisky.

When the Ferintosh Distillery was forced to close its doors in 1784 when the government introduced new and stricter taxes, the Scottish were deeply saddened – not only Robert Burns, but just about every whisky drinker on the island. At the time, Ferintosh was synonymous with first-class whisky. Some say it was because of the low retail price, but that is slander. Ferintosh had a distinctive, strong peat flavour, which drinkers saw as proof of quality. Ferintosh was Burns's salty sin. Not his alone, either; Sir Walter Scott also loved it, and it is said that Bonnie Prince Charlie, after his defeat by the 'bloody' English at Culloden, could only drown his sorrows in a series of Ferintosh whiskies.

Burns poured his heart out in a poem of 21 long stanzas in his near-impenetrable language, which is difficult to decipher. But it all comes down to this:

Thee, Ferintosh! O sadly lost!
Scotland lament frae coast to coast!

Whisky lovers did not immediately attribute Ferintosh's downfall to the taxes themselves, but rather to the servants of the law: the tax inspectors.

Burns, too, disliked the 'excise men' who snooped around the distilleries and were, in the opinion of every Scotsman, a species best kept at arm's length. To summarise, Burns wrote that people who collected taxes on alcohol and pursued bootleggers deserved to be taken away by the devil. After that, any sensible person would be dancing around happily.

In 'Scotch Drinks' he writes these lines:

They curst horse-leeches o' th' Excise,
Wha mak the whisky stells their prize!
Haud up thy han', Deil! ance, twice, thrice!

In plain speech: "You cursed horse-leeches of the Excise who take money from our whisky. Hands up!"

It may come as a surprise that this whisky fanatic became an excise inspector himself at 30. But his 'Scotch Drinks' were not intended to send those 'horse leeches' to the gallows, but rather an indictment of the poverty and squalor in which the ordinary Scot had to live in the late 18th century.

It was the same need for money that forced him to take a job as an 'exciseman'.

His farm did not provide the necessary pennies to support his wife and six scattered children.

In that capacity, he rode about three hundred kilometres a week on horseback across the country. He earned fifty pounds a year, plus fifty for each smuggler he apprehended and half the value of the kettles and goods seized. To give him credit, we must say that he only went after the 'big fish' and disregarded the smaller ones.

The noble whisky drinker.

Burns, too, disliked the `excise men' who snooped around the distilleries and were, in the opinion of every Scotsman, a species best kept at arm's length.

His songs in praise of whisky (which he called 'John Barleycorn') surpass his best love songs.

Inspiring bold John Barleycorn!
What dangers thou canst make us scorn!
Wi' tippeny, we fear nae evil;
Wi' usquabae, we'll face the devil!

And these are his immortal words: "Freedom and whisky gang together, take aff your dram!"

No wonder he will never be forgotten: on 25 January, the whole (whisky) world celebrates his birthday with Burns' Night, featuring lots of poetry and whisky, accompanied by haggis, neeps and tatties, and at the end everyone sings his 'Auld Lang Syne'.

Should auld acquaintance be forgot, and never brought to mind?
Should auld acquaintance be forgot, and days of auld lang syne?
For auld lang syne, my jo, for auld lang syne,
we'll tak a cup o' kindness yet, for auld lang syne.

No Scottish celebration would be complete without this farewell song. It has been translated into almost every language in the world.

Burns said (although we are almost sure that he was merely recording the words of an old Scottish song): Should we really forget all we have seen and all we have met? And stop remembering it? Let's raise a glass of friendship together:

For Auld Lang Syne... to the days of yore!
Come on, what are you waiting for?
Fill your 'cup o' kindness'!
For auld lang syne, my jo... To the days of yore!
Slàinte Mhath!

60 Slàinte Mhath

So Slàinte Mhath is simply the Gaelic equivalent of the French 'santé' and the German 'Gesundheit'. You shout it as you raise your glass. It is usually shortened to 'slanshe'. It is Scottish and Irish, but the spelling and pronunciation differs slightly between the two Gaelic languages. But no matter. By the way, it's not as widespread as you might think. Gaelic is not as ubiquitous as it once was. In the West and the Hebrides, there are said to be around 60,000 people who still understand the ancient Gaelic language – and that's not a lot. Moreover, those numbers are declining rapidly.

SLÀINTE MHATH

WHAT

Gaelic, loosely translated, 'good health'

PRONUNCIATION

Slansche va

WHERE

Ireland, some parts of Scotland and whisky clubs everywhere

In 2006, the Scottish government allocated more than £10 million to establish a Gaelic television station, BBC Alba, and to make the language compulsory again in some schools. Children's books were also published in the language for the first time. Even in some places where Gaelic has not been spoken for a long time, the language has been introduced as a new optional supplementary course in school. But none of this has helped much. The number of Gaelic speakers continues to dwindle, and the language is doomed to extinction.

But that doesn't change the fact that at tastings, we frequently shout 'slanshe va' in chorus. It's fun! And it sounds so Scottish.

We did some surveying of our own.

Glenelg is a tiny village on the west coast of Scotland, near Skye: no more than a few hundred people scattered across a wild and quiet part of Scotland.

Glenelg is my secret retreat when I have a lot of writing to do and need some peace and quiet. I rent a skipper's cottage ten metres from the ocean and three hundred metres from the only pub, the Glenelg Inn. You can also eat there; they even have some rooms to let if needed.

In the evening, you will encounter a quarter of your fellow villagers and all their border collies, who occasionally roam the pub chasing balls. Across the road is a small shop, which is more of 'a first-aid kit' for basic necessities. Apart from that, very little happens there. The only time you have to keep an eye out is on Thursdays around ten o'clock in the morning, because that's when the bin lorry passes by.

The first time I went there with Jan Bresseleers (my unpaid copy corrector), we, as newcomers, offered a drink for everyone. We raised our glasses and shouted 'slanshe va'.

After that, it was quiet in the pub for a while. The collies even seemed to forget their balls and simply stared at us. Stewart, a regular with a favourite seat at the corner of the bar, broke the silence with an understanding 'cheers'.

And then everyone joined in: "Cheers."

That's what you get when you want to pretend to be an insider.

So, in future, check first to see how familiar they are with your drinking habits at home – especially if you end up in a remote area of the UK.

In Wales, for example, where they call whisky 'chwisgi', you might want to stick to 'llonniannau' – at least if you know how to pronounce the two consecutive letters 'l'. Fortunately, eighty per cent of Welshmen speak plain English. It might be best to stick to 'cheers'.

I would also be careful on the Isle of Man, which also has King Charles III as its head of state, but is not part of the UK (nor the EU). In Manx, a language comparable to Irish and Scottish Gaelic, 'to your health' sounds like 'slaynt vie, bea veayn, beeal fliugh as baase ayns Mannin', but you can shorten it to 'slaynt vie', which you pronounce 'gflintvaai'.

Good to know before you go!

However, if you plan to explore the island by motorbike, you won't get far with your smatterings of Manx. The last person who spoke Manx daily was Ned Maddrell, and the islander is no more; he died in 1974. We do not know his last words, because those present could not understand what he was saying.

One wonders who he was talking to in Manx.

Perhaps he had a dog.

61 Penderyn I, Penderyn II, Penderyn III

PENDERYN I, PENDERYN II, PENDERYN III

WHAT

Three distilleries in one

NOTABLE

With three female master distillers

REMARKABLE

Five rare Faraday stills

I don't know how it happened, but as I drove to Penderyn Distillery at the foot of the Brecon Beacons in South Wales, I was suddenly reminded of Saint Teilo. Not that I often think of saints, quite the opposite, but I once read a story about this man who is said to have dwelled in this region. He was born around 500 in Penally, a bit further west. He must have been a strange fellow because the stories say that he once brought a wild, winged dragon to its knees and tied it to a rock in the sea off Brittany. He must have done more spectacular things, too; achieving sainthood is not that easy.

But the most striking thing about him is that there was only one Saint Teilo, but he is buried in three different places: at Penally, at Llandeilo Fawr and Llandaff. You mustn't think that these purported burial grounds have a scrap of Teilo here and another scrap there', no, all three locations claim a 'whole saint'. And so we find him three times in the (full) calendar of saints: on 9 February, 25 November and 29 November!

This is only possible in Wales.

No eating
No drinking
No smoking

And Penderyn proves it!
There is only one Penderyn Distillery, but there are three Penderyn Distilleries in Wales. The distillery proudly states on its website that this is a world record. Not only that, but they are apparently the only three distilleries to use Faraday stills and the only distillery to have an all-female master blender and master distiller. Well then!

Penderyn I

For more than a century, Wales did not have even one single distillery. But in 1998, four friends changed that. All it took was a pleasant evening in the Glencynon Inn pub in the village of Hirwaun. The four pooled their resources and formed the Welsh Whisky Company.

A vacant building for the distillery was quickly found in the neighbouring village of Penderyn (which also solved the problem of a good brand name). Even more fortunate was the search for a suitable still: a coppersmith was stuck with a finished still that he could not sell. No classic whisky still, it had been designed by Dr David Faraday, a descendant of the great 19th-century scientist Michael Faraday, specifically for a perfume factory: a combination of a still and a seven-plate column. But the boys had no problem with this; on the contrary, it allowed the entire distillation process to be carried out in one go, from wash to new spirit at 92% ABV (although at Penderyn, they stick to a maximum of 88%). And this still, it soon turned out, produced a fresh, light and fruity spirit.

The first Penderyn was bottled in 2004. A second, identical Faraday still was purchased in 2013 to meet growing demand, and two classic stills were added a year later. Inside the distillery, every square inch has been occupied with deliberate care.

Aista Phillips, Penderyn I's master blender, is originally from Lithuania; she has been at the heart of the whole process and praises the help she received from Dr Jim Swan, who helped get so many fledgling distilleries off the ground. (He died far too young in 2017.)

In addition to their Gold range (with the ornate bottles) and Dragon range (less decoratively bottled, apparently because the French market didn't want the ornate ones), they also launched the 'Royal Welsh Whisky', a tribute to the defunct Longoch distillery.

In all of this, she experimented with bourbon, Madeira, sherry, re-roasted wine casks, and ex-Islay casks for their lightly turfed whiskies.

But all that was about to change.

Penderyn II

Llandudno, where Penderyn built its second distillery, is a quintessential old English seaside town that still retains some of its former glory. In the nineteenth century, a little train brought in crowds of bathers. It was the place to be!

When we arrived on a Sunday morning, the once-bustling Lloyd Street looked deserted.

Llandudno is located on a small peninsula in North Wales, some two hundred and fifty kilometres (a four-hour drive) from the 'mother distillery' in the Brecon Beacons.

Dafydd Pesic-Smith, the manager of what is officially known as 'Penderyn Llandudno Lloyd Street Distillery', makes no bones about it: "We are still on the edge of tourist Wales, with Snowdonia very close by. Before, if you wanted to visit our distillery in the Brecon Beacons from here, you would spend a whole day on the road. Now, you have all the facilities on the doorstep, and people are taking advantage of them."

The business started in May 2021 in a fully and tastefully restored 1882 school building: the Old Board School. There's not much whisky atmosphere outside the building, apart from the stacked casks in a corner, one for each letter of the company name. A side road leads to the actual entrance of the visitor centre, which immediately sets the tone for the whole place: modern, open and colourful.

Unlike the 'old' distillery, there is only one Faraday still at this location. And they'll have to make do.

Dafydd: "Up to now, the peat accents in our whiskies come from old Laphroaig quarter casks. But from now on, we are creating the first Penderyn whisky from peated malt! Now, all our whisky will be peated whisky." That means we'll have to wait a few years more to taste a real Penderyn II.

Penderyn III

Building a new distillery forty kilometres from the first was not based on a desire to attract more tourists. Rather, it was prompted by an urgent need to boost production. The 'old' Penderyn produces 400,000 litres yearly, but they needed double that. And that is exactly what the brand-new Penderyn Swansea Copperworks Distillery is about to deliver.

Swansea was once known as 'Copperopolis'. The Swansea Hafod-Morfa Copperworks, which opened in 1808, was the largest in the world, covering fifty acres and employing two thousand workers. Copper ore was brought in from all over the world. The copperworks was full of heavy machinery, hellish noise, heat and pollution. After the First World War, the company fell into disrepair, and the whole site was a sad ruin by 1960. Many of the buildings had crumbled into nothing, and the rest were overgrown.

Half a century later, the Welsh Government put up half a million pounds to spruce things up. And in 2019, the National Lottery Heritage Fund put in another four million (matched by money from several investors) to start the renovation. Penderyn's plan to create a third distillery immediately took shape.

What was once the engine room of the distillery is now called the Distillery Hall: a large, high hall with lots of Victorian wrought iron and ample daylight. This building houses the entire distilling operation (which again includes two Faraday stills and two classic Scotch stills). You enter via the Visitor Centre and the Copper Tunnel: a winding covered passageway that evokes the old factory's atmosphere (and sounds). Up a mirrored staircase and through a sea of bottles, you enter the state-of-the-art tasting room and, a little further on, the surprising Whisky Bar.

The first drops of the new spirit were captured in mid-September 2023, and they are now ready to double Penderyn's production.

62 AI whisky

> AI WHISKY
>
> WHAT
>
> Whisky based on an Artificial Intelligence recipe
>
> SIGNIFICANCE
>
> Innovative and promising for the future?
>
> WHERE
>
> In Sweden, where alcohol advertising is banned, everyone tries to make it into the newspaper anyway.

I know a Japanese restaurant in The Hague that I would have recommended to you back in the day. I used to go there every year during the International Whisky Festival. It was always a feast. We sat by an open kitchen where a dozen or more chefs were preparing an endless number of small dishes. You could order six dishes at a time in several rounds, as much as you could eat for one fixed price. And it was always brought to you with a smile by an enthusiastic, chatty waiter or waitress. Delicious!

The last time I was there, the lady who used to welcome you at the door and escort you to your table was absent. One of the chefs responded to my dilly-dallying by pointing to an empty table. Satisfied that I understood, he raised his thumb. The table was not set, but a tablet was in the corner by the window. I told my wife, "Not very wise to forget your tablet in a restaurant."

After ten minutes of staring around, I suddenly noticed the same cook looking in my direction and pointing at the tablet. I took the tablet, and I got his thumbs-up.

With some trepidation, I pressed the ingenious start button on the tablet. Immediately, we saw all the food and drinks you could get, which were nicely displayed. You just had to click on a dish and say how many you wanted. For a try, we selected six each and then clicked 'SEND'.

You won't believe me, but less than two minutes later, a young lady, not a robot... a real lady, brought all the dishes. And she could talk, too; she said very clearly "enjoy".

There are moments in your life when you wish you were far away, even in the busiest street of Shanghai, with a vegetarian burger in your hand.

And then... a frightening thought suddenly popped into my head, one that gavc me goosebumps: imagine if those IT guys were to start messing with my whisky one day!

But my wife, who knows better than anyone how to reassure me, immediately said, "Don't be silly."

Not much later, I was struck by a figurative bolt of lightning. On page 1 of its 'Food&Drink' supplement, 'The Scotsman' ran a heart-stopping headline: "How Artificial Intelligence is being used in the whisky industry, and what it could mean for the future"!

On my empty stomach! I hadn't even showered yet.

Mackmyra, the Swedish distillery, has partnered with Microsoft and Finland's Fourkind to design a whisky that will conquer all drinkers. Of course, Angela D'Orazia, Mackmyra's master blender, kept a close eye on things, but the first say came from... artificial intelligence. I should have capitalised that, but it hurts too much.

The Modern Cry—"JOHNNIE WALKER"

Like the "pick-me-up" of olden time, that on the street was bought, its virtues are applauded by those who know "what's what." All experts agree that there are periods when whisky is at its best; our experts contend there are three. Choose for yourself——— Johnnie Walker "White Label," 6 years old. Johnnie Walker "Red Label," 10 years old. Johnnie Walker "Black Label," 12 years old.

Every bottle bears this label:———" Guaranteed same quality throughout the world."

JOHN WALKER & SONS, Ltd., Scotch Whisky Distillers, KILMARNOCK.

Modern approach with 'The Modern Cry' in 1912 ↑

Let me briefly summarise what these Swedes did.

They took 75 recipes for whiskies they had created in the past. They put them into a computer, along with a massive amount of data about customer preferences, awards won, newspaper clippings and market phenomena.

Again, you won't believe it, but the computer spit out no less than 70,000,000 possible new recipes in less than a flash.

As a whisky lover, that might make you giddy.

Or possibly furious.

But Angela D'Orazia kept her calm and, by eliminating the many suggested recipes that were simply idiotic, reduced the number to 30. And a little later to five.

One of these five, recipe 36, was then produced: the INTELLIGENS. The first five thousand bottles are selling out fast, and a second edition is already on the market. Not bad!

Although I once took the holy oath never to write tasting notes in my books, I will do it this time, even though I haven't tasted that unique Intelligens yet.

But you would certainly have blamed me if I had kept these revolutionary results from you. Mackmyra's website says it all: "An elegant, fruity whisky with notes of toffee, creamy vanilla, pear, apple, white pepper and a hint of oak."

If that's not new to the whisky world, I don't know what is!

After that, the AI whisky story went quiet. Gradually, the nagging sense of dread disappeared from people's minds, and was eventually forgotten. And those are the most dangerous moments.

Diageo opened the Johnny Walker Experience on Edinburgh's Princes Street two years later, a brilliant tribute to the drink of our gods. Diageo spent £185 million on it: a Disney World for any whisky fanatic. Colourful, flashy... beautiful.

But as always, the danger is never far away.

On entering, you first have to work your way through a 'relatively simple' Flavour Finder quiz. This looks fun and entertaining, but nothing could be further from the truth: what you disclose there is irrevocably passed on to (brace yourself!) a computer loaded with artificial intelligence. As a result, the computer immediately tells you which colour wristband to wear, which you have to keep on your wrist throughout your Journey of Flavour Tour.

If you are offered a whisky or whisky cocktail later on in the tour, it will be different from your neighbour's, even if you wanted it to be the same. No, based on your quiz answers, you'll get what the computer said you would prefer – thanks to AI.

It's all well-intentioned, of course. But there you are. Look... talk to your neighbour; he might also be curious about what your 'favourite whisky' tastes like. Just swap! Human intelligence at work.

I may have exaggerated a bit, but don't worry, it's not all that bad. Just this morning, I read in the paper that Microsoft (which is getting rid of some of its copywriters and replacing them with AI) has advised in a new AI-authored article that readers looking for a good restaurant should visit the excellent food bank in Ottawa – a must-see!

There is still hope for humans!

63 One for the road

It is unclear why this pernicious custom originated and who is responsible for it. Some say it dates back centuries to a time when travellers had to cover long distances on horseback and had little opportunity to eat or drink on the route. To fend off discomfort, they would take something 'for the road'. But that's not quite right! Although you took it with you, you didn't drink or eat it before you left!

ONE FOR THE ROAD

ABBREVIATED

OFTR

MEANS

A 'last' alcoholic drink offered before leaving

SYNONYM

One for the gather

Others (probably English) insist that the expression was used in previous centuries to give the condemned a chance to drink 'one for the road' in the last pub on their way to the noose or the scaffold. That sounds credible, but you'll have to excuse me if I don't believe it. A pat on the back and "Come on man, keep your head up, we're going to take another one!"? Knowing the English... No. Mind you, I don't mean that in a negative sense.

Others point out that it should be 'one for the rope': the ship's crew had one last drink before boarding and pulling up the ropes. Mooring ROPE... Get it? I don't believe that one, either. Those guys had certainly something on board, didn't they? And it wasn't just water.

That brings us to Eric Partridge. This New Zealand-British lexicographer (who was a professor at several universities in the UK), a specialist in English jargon, will surely know. We can no longer ask him directly, since he died in 1979, but he fortunately wrote various books in which he expertly dissected the English language. According to him, the term originated with an early 20th-century travelling salesman who would knock back one last drink after an evening of drinking, before literally 'hitting the road' to see more customers.

Sorry, I guess we'll just have to accept it.

So we are left with 'one for the road': drink one and then go home. But not in every pub in the world.

That leaves 'one for the gather', an alternative option in which drinkers in an advanced state of inebriation attempt to demonstrate that the last glass is only meant to be thrown up along with some previous ones. You know me well enough to appreciate that I don't want to explore this concept any further.

So we are left with 'one for the road': drink one and then go home.

But not in every pub in the world.

As I wandered around Britain, I discovered several places where 'one for the road' meant much more: in some cases, it was even a 'goodbye forever'.

On the front of the 'Ye Olde Trip to Jerusalem' pub in Nottingham, it says 'Since 1189'. And rumour has it that the Crusaders set off from this pub to the Holy Land to attack the Moors. That last drink in 'Ye Olde Trip' was a real 'one for the road', at least if the date and accompanying rumour are valid.

To make things even more credible, it is also said that the pub itself is that old, but the entrance dates from the seventeenth century. That was a flourishing century for pilgrimages, so it is possible that pilgrims left from here for the Holy Land, and had their last 'one for the road' before setting out.

I do wonder if the pilgrims drank alcohol. I've seen pictures of people on their way to Santiago de Compostela, and they don't look like heavy drinkers. But 'one for the road' refers not only to drink, but also to food. So they could have taken along a piece of bread for the journey.

I don't know exactly how long bread remains edible, or how long it takes to walk from Nottingham to Jerusalem, but I'm sure it must be a reassuring feeling to close the door on 'Ye Olde Trip' knowing that you have 'one for the road' in your rucksack.

At the California Country Inn in Ivybridge, Devon, 'one for the road' was more like 'until never'. This delightful pub dates back to the 14th century and was a regular stagecoach stop for many years, where fortune-seekers gathered to catch the stagecoach to Plymouth and embark on a ship headed westward to the New World.

Finally, remember that exclaiming 'one for the road' before driving home is strictly forbidden in some countries, and increasingly frowned upon in others (not least various states in the US). Indeed, a lot has changed since that first 'one for the road'.

Going home was very different then than it is now. Back then, you could rely on your trusty four-legged friend. Your horse would have waited patiently for you outside, not even bothering to check where you'd been for so long, and then, knowing the way, would have taken you quietly and completely safely to your bed while you dozed blissfully in the saddle.

I am still looking for a GPS that can match that.

63.5 Cheers

CHEERS

WHAT

The Buffalo Theory

AUTHOR

Cliff Clavin

AUDIENCE

Norman and friends

At the end of the last century, NBC broadcast a comedy series with the promising title 'Cheers' on US television. Viewers were immediately assured that a fine drink or a good glass of beer would never be far away. More than 270 episodes were produced, and several foreign broadcasters later picked up the series. It was a huge success.

The setting for 'Cheers' was a tavern and restaurant that still stands on Beacon Street in Boston. Unlike the real 'Cheers', the clientele of the TV bar was a little more flamboyant.

The waitresses were real-life prototypes, and a client who was a psychiatrist unmistakably had a relationship with one of them.

One frequent guest at the bar was Cliff Clavin, a well-spoken joker who never failed to demonstrate the richness of his 'intellectual baggage'. He devised the 'Buffalo Theory', which he explained to his best friend and bar mate Norm in his usual smooth style.

His theory is worth pondering. Sitting at the bar in a lively pub like Cheers, the Buffalo Theory sounds quite logical.

I'll leave it up to your best judgment. Just listen.

Cliff Clavin says, "A herd of buffalo can only move as fast as the slowest buffalo. And when the herd is hunted, the slowest and weakest at the back are killed first. This natural selection is good for the herd as a whole, as the speed and health of the whole group continue to improve as the weakest members are regularly killed.

"In the same way, the human brain can only work as fast as the slowest brain cells. Excessive alcohol consumption is known to kill brain cells. But, of course, the weakest brain cells die first. In this way, regular alcohol consumption eliminates the weaker brain cells, making the brain a faster and more efficient machine."

Conclusion: someone who drinks a lot always knows better than the rest!

Look, you obviously expect me to offer some response to that claim, and quite right, too! Indeed, it is unacceptable that such statements can be made with impunity in a well-researched, science-based whisky book like this one.

However, from the start, the publisher limited this book to 63.5 chapters by contract, and this one, as you will have noticed, is the last chapter. The half chapter.

Sorry about that!

But there are worse things in the world.

Have another wee dram now.

According to Cliff, you'll understand better after that.

www.lannoo.com

Register on our web site and we will regularly send you a newsletter with information about new books and interesting, exclusive offers.

Text: Fernand Dacquin
Cover design: Studio Lannoo
Cover photograph: Kris Vlegels, papil bvba
Photograph author: Hervé Debaene
Photography: istock (p. 2, 4, 13, 16, 20, 24, 32, 36, 47, 49, 50, 51, 57, 59, 71, 81, 84, 88, 90, 102, 109, 116, 119, 125, 130, 132, 161, 162, 166, 172, 174, 178, 180, 183, 184, 186, 194, 196, 200, 213, back cover), author's property (p. 8, 15, 19, 28, 31, 52, 55, 63, 64, 69, 81, 87, 95, 96, 104, 111, 115, 126, 129, 135, 137, 151, 154, 155, 166, 167, 168, 176, 183, 186, 191, 193, 196, 198, 205, 206, 210, 214), Kris Vlegels (p. 1), Alamy (p. 72), Story of Leicester (p. 42), Hervé Debaene (p. 6), Wikimedia Commons (p. 12, 21, 23, 25, 27, 32, 38, 41, 49, 56, 61, 66, 75, 77, 78, 93, 99, 101, 112, 120, 122, 139, 141, 143, 147, 153, 171, 188, 213)
Design: Studio Lannoo
Typesetting: Kaatigo

Invoegen: For the use of third-party photos, efforts have been made to identify the rights holders. Should you nevertheless come across photos of which you are the rights holder, please contact us at redactielifestyle@lannoo.be
If you have observations or questions, please contact our editorial office: redactielifestyle@lannoo.com

D/2024/45/495 – NUR 447
ISBN 978-94-014-4044-8